Digital

Divide

TV Books

NEW YORK

Digital Divide

Computers and Our Children's Future

David B. Bolt

Ray A. K. Crawford

Copyright © 2000 by TV Books LLC

Library of Congress Cataloging-in-Publication Data
Bolt, David, 1954–
    Digital divide : computers & our children's future / by David Bolt, Ray Crawford.
        p. cm.
    ISBN 1-57500-086-5
    1. Education—United States—Data processing. 2. Computer-assisted instruction—Social aspects—United States. 3. Educational equalization—United States. 4. Computers and children. I. Crawford, Ray, 1954– II. Title.
    LB1028.43.B64 2000
    371.33'4—dc21

                                                            99-088058

The publisher has made every effort to secure permission to reproduce copyrighted material and would like to apologize should there have been any errors or omissions.

TV Books, L.L.C.
1619 Broadway, Ninth Floor
New York, NY 10019
www.tvbooks.com

Interior design by Rachel Reiss
Manufactured in the United States of America

Dedication

To my wife, Sue Ellen McCann, and to my son, Nate Bolt.
They inspire me in all that I do. —David Bolt

To my best friend and greatest Love, Karla, and to my
angel kitten Circe, always in my heart and in my thoughts.
—Ray Crawford

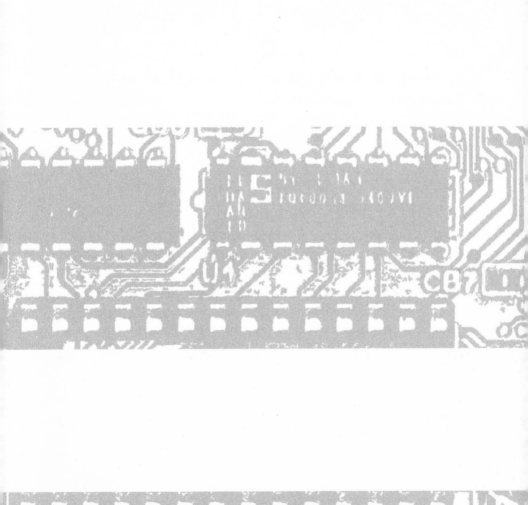

Contents

Between the idea
And the reality
Between the motion
And the act
Falls the Shadow

—T. S. Eliot

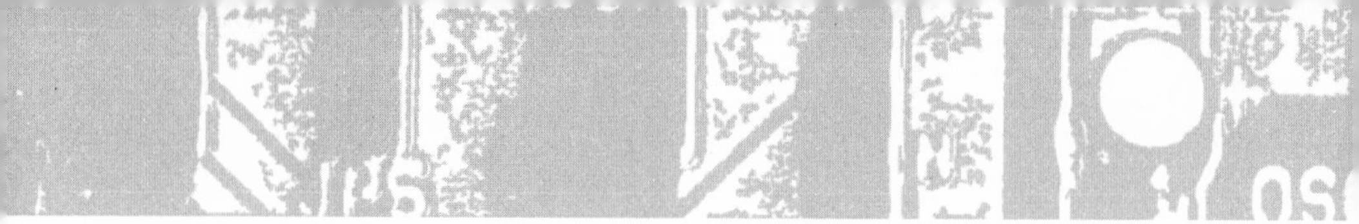

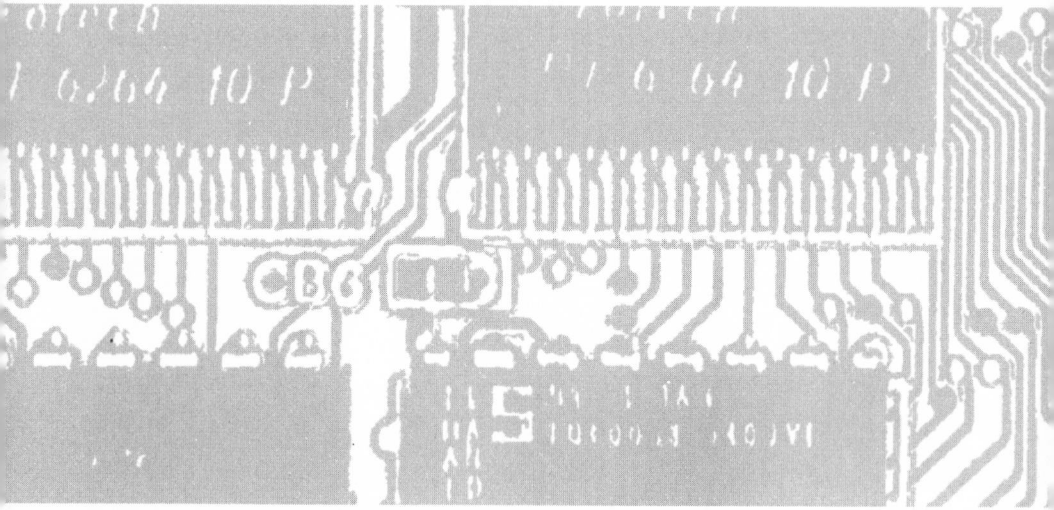
6264 10 P
CB6

Acknowledgments

I would like to thank my wife and partner, Sue Ellen McCann, for all that she did to bring the "Digital Divide" series and book to fruition. Sue Ellen, an executive producer at KQED (San Francisco PBS) where she produces programs about technology among other things, wrote the original proposals with me, produced one of the episodes of the series, and read materials for the book. My son, Nate Bolt, provided the inspiration for the series; in fact, he's fond of saying I stole the idea from him. Nate is an "Information Architect" for Clearink.com, where he analyzes human-computer interaction for complex websites. Without my wife and son, none of this would have happened.

The staff at Studio Miramar, Colleen Wilson, and Kathleen Michaud have been extremely helpful in this process. I would also like to give a special thanks to all the seasoned filmmakers and researchers who helped find and craft the eloquent stories in the series and book: producer/directors David L. Brown, Debra Chasnoff, Helen Cohen, Sue Ellen McCann, and Lorna Thomas; associate producers Valerie Lapin Ganley, Myra Levy, and Gretchen Stoeltje; co-producers Michelle Halsell and Rachel Raney; and editors Augie Cinquengrana, Darren Kloomok, Elizabeth Long, Bob Sarles, Kate Stilley, and Wendy Wank.

Another special thanks goes to the capable team who lent their special talents to the production: narrators Queen Latifah and Regina Taylor, writers Charlie Pearson and Oriana Zill, production manager Kathleen Michaud, and coordinating producer Colleen Wilson. The series was funded by and produced in association with the Independent Television Service.

I would like to extend a special thanks to the individuals who allowed us to film their stories and who shared their insights with us in the series and the book: Ernest Adams, Kevin Allard-Mendelson, Carmen Alvarez, Gabby and Valerie Baeza, Dominic Bannister, Stephen Baumann, Micheleann Beardsley, Victor and Vincent Bell, Marc R. Benioff, Andrew Blau, Theresa Boyd, Patricia S. Bransford, Carol Burger, Laura Burges, Jennifer and Jessica Cantu, Norman Cooper, Gary Dalton, Virginia Davis, Marilu Delgado Houshmand, Vickie N. Dunlevy, Sidra Durst, Travis Eliason, Karen Elinich, Yvette Fagen, Allan Fisher, Lelar Floyd, Ted Fujimoto, B. Keith Fulton, Faith Galvan, Rachel Gonzalez, Douglas Goodkin, Laura Groppe, Janet Harkins, Esther Hartwell, Jane Healy, Terry Hiner, Donna Hoffman, Ph.D., Larry Irving, Michio Kaku, Madeline Lacovara, Brenda Laurel, Kep Lim, Bruce Lincoln, Anthony Lopez, Diane Luffy, John Mack, Nancie S. Martin, Elena McFadden, Sophie Metts, Trish Millines Dziko, Mark Morrison, Tariq Muhammad, Douglas Nelson, Linda Novack, Todd Ollendyke, Peggy Orenstein, Hilary Pennington, Iris and Krystal Perez, Lana Perry, Alison Reed, Robert Reich, Kristi Rennebohm Franz, Steven Rice, Jeremy Rifkin, Geraldo Rivera, William Rukeyser, Jo Sanders, Sarah

Schulman, Sofia Shaikh, Heidi Swanson, Janese Swanson, Cassandra Van Buren, Carmen Vega-Rivera, Omar Wasow, Cheryl Williams, Starla Williams, and Anastasia Zita.

A special tip of the hat to Don Tapscott, the writer who first coined the phrase "digital divide"! And finally, ciao to our friend and colleague, Augie Cinquengrana (1940–1999) who brought his warmth and intelligence to the editing of the series.

—*David Bolt*

There are far too many people to acknowledge in as short a space as I have here. Everyone I've met, and been friends with, loved, or disliked has influenced me to one degree or another in one way or another along the path of my life. While it is always difficult to publicly acknowledge some without acknowledging all, it is impossible not to give some accolades, so I will name relatively few individually but remember all of you in my heart.

First and foremost, my family, who have always been supportive of this and all my other projects. To my dad and mom, Raymond and Joyce Kanarr; my sister Karen and her family Bill, Justin, Cory, and Zachary; my sister Wendy; my aunts Joan, Diana, Marilyn, and Ina Mae and uncles Roger, Fred, Warren, Michael, and Erwin; and all of my cousins, especially Dan, Janet, Nancy; as well as to my second family: my brother-in-law Miles and his family Kathy, Ian, and Paige; Bob and Marlene; Cliff and Burne, thanks for being there and being family.

I'd like to acknowledge the many teachers and others who have made such a difference in my life, and taught me to think for myself. I'd like to give a lot of credit to Barbara Davis-

Kerbel, Jack McGrath, Reva Field, Al Candia, Thom Blake, Harvey Witman, and Ed Leigh for starting me on this long, strange trip; to Kathy Bovino, Sheila Schneider, Ben Bloch, and Ursula Buono for believing in me long before I believed in myself; to Jack Crawford, Richard Hathaway, Ken Skelton, Larry Sullivan, and Bob Waugh at the State University of New York at New Paltz for helping me along the road to becoming a person who could even consider writing; and to Gwen, Iris, Paul, and Renee for helping me in the evolution of my work life.

Finally, I couldn't end this without an expansive acknowledgment of my friends, without whom my life would be very different and nowhere near as wonderful as it is. All I can say to Will and Marti; Bonnie and Carl; John; Dianne; Jeannette and David; David and Sue Ellen; Bill, Deb, and Ben; Teri; Deneen; Carter; Bob and Linda; Michael, Julie, and Dara; Bob and Joy; Jeff; David and Maria; Joe and Karen; Jim; David and Aiqin; Harald; Lauren; Steve; Harvey; Lynette; Laurie; Pam; Harvey; Sal; Paul; and anyone else I might (in my decrepitude) have forgotten, is thanks for all the love, time, and memories, past, present, and future. Last of all, to all those people I knew and loved in the Classes of 1970, 1971, and 1972 at Commack High School South, and in the Classes of 1975 and 1976 at Alfred University and the State University of New York at New Paltz: wherever you are, whatever you're doing, I think about you and wish you well. And I wish you'd get in touch sometime!

—Ray Crawford

Introduction

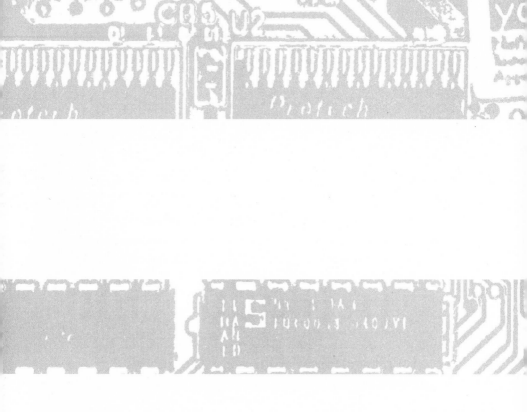

When I first started developing the "Digital Divide" television series for PBS in 1997, there were very few folks who were familiar with the term. I spent a fair amount of time trying to explain the concept of the divide to funders, PBS, and community organizations. Several years later the term has entered the popular lexicon. More importantly, activism around the divide is at an all-time high and growing. Hopefully this book and series, along with the website and our outreach efforts, will reach even more folks with the story of the digital divide and what it means for our future.

A quarter-century ago there was a prevailing notion in our society that a young person fresh out of school could enter a trade or vocation and spend their life as a securely employed blue-collar worker. Now, the reality is far different. The lack of exposure to technology, at home and in the classroom, dooms millions of American youths to low-paid, insecure jobs at the margins of our economy. At the same time, wealthy children in private schools are reaping the rewards of immersion in the new technologies: their homes have DSL internet connections and their summer jobs involve designing websites or writing computer code. Far from being a panacea for a bright future, technology looms as a barrier to the American Dream for many, perhaps most, of our young people.

I think one question to keep in mind vis-à-vis digital technology is the issue of access (I call it the "quantitative" side of the equation) on the one hand, and the issue of content (e.g., the "qualitative") on the other. That is why this book and the "Digital Divide" series examine both quantitative and qualitative aspects of digital technology, ranging from the curricular role of computers in elementary schools to the growth of technological jobs in the American economy. We must focus first on access issues to ensure that as many people as possible have access to digital technology. Access, however, as this series and book point out, is just the starting point of a broader discussion about the role of computers in our culture. It would be a mistake to blindly advocate computers for all without also having a discussion about how best to use these tools.

Words like "cyberspace," "internet," "multimedia," "on-line," "e-mail," and "microprocessor" seem commonplace in our media. Yet the stark reality is that tens of millions of Americans are not at all conversant with digital tools, and tens of millions more have only a passing familiarity with the most basic of applications: word processing and e-mail. Many people without digital skills know that their options may be increasingly bleak as a result of this lack of knowledge. Digital technology impacts directly on the proverbial bottom line in each of our lives.

American television is awash with self-congratulatory shows on the wonders of digital technology. Every major broadcast network and cable consortium now has at least one weekly or daily program cheerleading for it. I think many of us acknowledge the important role that computers already play in several areas of our lives: we write on them, correspond on them, edit our videos with them; they drive our cameras and our sound systems, create our graphics, and on and on. Digital technology has certainly changed my work in terms of all the steps of a television program's life from conception through pre-production, production, post-production, and distribution.

What the series and book represent is critical thinking about digital technology that is also conversant with the tools of that technology. I have the ability to do this as my experience comes not only from producing television programs but also from creating large, innovative technological programs. I recruited and oversaw technological staff as the Executive Director of the Bay Area Video Coalition, at Skywalker Ranch as the Production Director for the George Lucas Educational Foundation, and as the Vice-President of Technology for the California College of Arts & Crafts. I have also been a television producer throughout the past two decades. This cumulative experience gives me a historic perspective on the development of technology over the past twenty years.

Yet, while digital technology has changed the way we live our lives, there are many unresolved issues. Even if we gave everyone a computer or internet connection tomorrow, there would still be many issues to resolve in terms of their use. It is not only a question of trying to figure out which communications technologies will dominate the landscape; it is also a question of assessing the human dimension of the historic transition to digital technology.

This book examines the divide in terms of its principal components: education, employment, race, and gender. Each of these aspects of the divide is unique, but they each lead up to a simple question—what will our roles be in the new, increasingly digital, economy? Following these four sections are profiles of the experts interviewed for the book and series, as well as a list of internet resources for further research. Finally, a set of five appendices provide statistical information on the digital divide, more of which can be found in the U.S. Department of Commerce's study *Falling Through the Net*.

Digital Divide—the book and the series—is one of the first to focus on asking hard questions about the role of digital technology in our lives. It is a must for every adult who worries about the digital future and for every student in America who questions his or her role in the Information Age. It is for every parent who searches for appropriate software for his or her child. It is for anyone who worries that they are being left behind because they don't adequately use a computer or internet connection at work or at home.

David Bolt
January 2000

1

Teaching Our Children Well

The public-school student of 1899 would not have had very much trouble fitting into the classroom of 1979. Despite changes in educational policy and advances in both our understanding of the learning process and knowledge of the world around us, the educational process did not differ notably in that eighty-year span. A knowledgeable educator at the front of the room, books containing the accumulated wisdom to be imparted, and hand-written exercises intended to inculcate the material to be learned were a major part of the experience that spanned generations of students, whatever their socioeconomic background.

A student from 1979, however, might not fit so easily into the classroom world of today. The last twenty years have seen a tremendous leap forward in the use of technology in classrooms, creating a different kind of educational experience for some students—but not, by any means, for all. Access to this technology, around which much of our educational system is becoming based, is not equally available to all students, is not handled equally well by all educators, and is not equally useful to everyone in education as it is presently structured.

This is the educational essence of the digital divide.

The arena of education in our nation is being altered by the introduction of computer and connectivity technology—the "wiring" of our schools. As this technology is introduced into the classroom, it can alter the way students are taught. It is important, therefore, to explore some of the fundamental concerns about introducing this technology, as well as its educational applications. There is an increasing disparity between schools and students with and without significant access to this technology, but access to technology itself is only one of many issues involved. In the world of today, more than at any time in the past century, much of a student's educational experience depends on that student's socioeconomic background. It has nothing to do with the student's intelligence, learning ability, or industriousness. Rather, it has to do with whether or not the student has access to technology, access to the information made available by that technology, and access to educators trained in integrating that technology and information into the educational experience.

U.S. PUBLIC EDUCATION ENCOMPASSES many different realities, depending upon many variables, including state requirements and curricula, educator licensing requirements, and the funding available to schools. In the area of computer and communications technologies, though, there are some commonalities. The majority of public schools still don't have directly allocated funds for telecommunications and don't have adequate infrastructure to support the technology being touted and dispensed by the computer industry and the government. Of the remaining schools, most do not have adequate funds for the maintenance and support of the equipment that they have managed to obtain. Even if adequate provision has been made for this (and it rarely is), the seemingly insurmountable obstacle of integrating this mass of equipment into a meaningful curriculum—including the significant teacher training required—still looms large.

Educators nationwide are faced with a set of continuing challenges, including overcrowded classrooms, poorly maintained facilities, uneven support, and insufficient pay scales and benefits packages. Now, in addition to their continuing mandated education requirements, teachers find themselves in the position of having to learn a wide variety of new technology-related skills to meet the social expectations of the Information Age: the use of computers, the use of a variety of software packages on computers, the use of the internet, and elementary troubleshooting techniques to offset the lack of comprehensive technical support. They are also expected to be able to convey this knowledge to their students, a group (like educators) ranging from the technophilic to the technophobic. Elena McFadden, a first grade teacher at Hoover Elementary School in Redwood City, California, is, in many ways, a typical educator trying to do her best with limited resources. "I took the computer class that teachers are required to take for their credentials, and I don't feel I received any training adequate to making me able to teach computers any better than when I walked into the class," Ms. McFadden noted. "You can't buy a bunch of computers and not train teachers to use them, and expect education and learning to go on."

Ms. McFadden is not alone in her views. As Program Director for the Markle Foundation, a private non-profit philanthropy that focuses on emerging technologies, Andrew Blau is one of the nation's preeminent specialists in education technology. While he has seen evidence that access to the technology in America's classrooms has improved, bringing the richest and the poorest schools closer together, he still feels that there are fundamental problems in the way computer technology is being brought into the classroom. "Our research suggests that it's access to trained teachers that makes the most difference in the lives of the kids," he says. "So, while the programs that exist to help poor schools get access to technology do appear to be having some effect, what we're not yet able to address is access to the one thing that seems to make the biggest difference, and that is trained teachers."

Teacher training has always been the central aspect of traditional educational methodologies, and remains so today. What is beginning to change is the way in which educators are taught, utilizing the new technologies that have taken center stage in the educational arena, a process that affords an opportunity for the educational establishment as a whole to engage in self-examination. "One opportunity that the introduction of computers in the classroom offers us," notes Mr. Blau, "is the opportunity to rethink what it is that teachers should be able to do in the classroom. What are we training them? How are we supporting them?"

The downside to this is that, as in many other fields, those instructing the next generation of educators are sometimes among the last to embrace change. Rather than seeing the new technologies as a way to look at the world with new eyes, some post-secondary instructors in education, and educators themselves, view the introduction of these technologies as a threat to their established educational methodologies. It may even be possible that, after putting in all of the time and effort needed to acquire this new skill set, many educators might re-examine their commitment to the teaching profession, precipitating a flight of many of the best and the brightest from the profession.

The picture remains bleak. In 1999, the Department of Education published the results of a survey of over thirty-five hundred of the nation's educators that asked about their facility with computer technology. Of those interviewed, only about 20 percent reported that they were "very well prepared" in using computer technology in the classroom, although approximately four-fifths of the educators indicated that they had some training in computers and related technology. Only those teachers who had received significant amounts of computer training felt that it helped their ability to use the computer in the classroom. Secretary of Education Richard Riley was not pleased with the survey results, stating that "teacher education and professional development programs are not addressing the realities found in today's classrooms. . . . One-shot workshops . . . carry little relevance to teachers' work in the classroom."

This view was reinforced by a study conducted jointly by the Milken Exchange on Educational Technology and the International Society for Technology in Education (ISTE), showing that most teacher-training programs treat computer technology as an adjunct to the curriculum, and not as a central feature. The study further indicated that teacher-training programs are not showing student educators how to effectively incorporate computer technology into their teaching methodology.

It is not enough to simply drop a bunch of computers into a classroom and walk away. It may not even be enough to completely wire an entire school district, train teachers in the use of the technology, and get students involved in using the computers thus made available. Such research indicates the need for a long, hard look at where educational technology is going. It is important to examine the situation that teachers find themselves in, and to ask whether this isn't another situation of tossing technology at a problem and asking the human factor to make adjustments.

Many of the issues surrounding the role of education in the Information Age were anticipated by former Labor Secretary Robert Reich in his 1991 book *The Work of Nations*. In it he criticized the nation's educational system for failing to provide an environment where general problem-solving and learning skills are taught and learned. He was dismayed by the lack of creativity in teaching and learning and the "simplification of reality" in educational settings, as though life in the real world were a linear series of events, each leading inevitably to the next—"a tour through history or geography or science typically has a fixed route." He attacked the prepackaged nature of lesson plans and textbooks that left no room for exploration, the discovery of greater meanings, or self-expression on the part of students. Speaking at the very beginning of the Information Age, Mr. Reich believed that current educational methodology would leave our children ill-prepared for success in what he styled the "new economy."

In general, none of the Mr. Reich's criticisms have been addressed. Eight years later, many of America's educational institutions are still trying to shoehorn computer technology directly into standardized and outdated curricula. The federal government seems to be proceeding with a program perhaps best characterized as "doing something, even if it's the wrong something" in pressing for the wiring of all of America's public classrooms by the year 2000. They may well achieve this goal, as figures released in late 1998 by the National Center for Education Statistics show that 89 percent of schools were connected to the internet and 51 percent of all classrooms were as well. The figures also indicate that these installations appear to be bridging one aspect of the digital divide. "We're making significant strides to get technology to the place where children learn—the classroom," said Richard Riley. "The 'digital divide' is closing in our nation's schools, but we have to close the continuing divide in our nation's classrooms." Unfortunately, there has been no equally dramatic announcement that a coherent body of thought, in the form of a national plan or even dialogue for using or assessing the effectiveness of these technologies, has been formed—what are we to do with all of that computer and communications technology once it is in place? The repercussions of this titanic head-on collision between the traditional model of education and the useful integration of technology in the classroom will reverberate well into the new millennium.

There are still many questions about the role of education in the Information Age, issues pertaining to selection of technology for the schools, proper use of the technology once it's in place, and the proper allocation of funds for computer-related technology. The indicators show that there is a direct correlation between the economic status of a public school and the amount of computer technology and support in that school. While technological support is not the be all and end all of education, it is certainly, as Andrew Blau points out, a head start in the race for the careers of the digital future. "Computers are not a silver bullet for whatever may be ailing public education today," he said. "Computers are tools. And the challenge is to make sure that we don't become slaves to our tools. If we're already wiring America's classrooms, we have a choice: either that we leave it totally to the market resources that each school district has, or we say, 'This is a set of tools that develop and cultivate a set of expertise that we want all kids to have'—that it becomes the new baseline for what it means to have basic educational skills that we want kids to leave high school with."

The major social pitfall of adopting the former option, according to Blau, is that those who initially have a leg up by virtue of their socioeconomic circumstances will have an even greater advantage at the end of their education, including a facility with technology and its vocabulary. As well, they will have a far better understanding of how the Information Age "works," in terms of knowledge about the available opportunities, the mechanism of wealth creation in the new age, and the new sociopolitical interactions being engendered by this technology. This is not a question of newer school texts or better football uniforms, it is literally a social fulcrum point that we as a nation have come to which will determine the face of our society well into the next century.

Blau further indicates the responsibilities that society must take on if we choose a path of equal access to, and equal educational experience, with this new technology: "If we go the other way and we say, 'These are the new tools of opportunity,' then we have a heavy burden. One burden is to make sure that they're used effectively, that they come in the package that will make this a wise investment. And two, that we take those steps that will make sure that we don't increase the gap, that we help the kids who need the help to get access to the tools that will allow them to take advantage of the opportunities they can make for themselves."

MOST OF US HAVE BECOME CONVINCED that, for better or worse, a person must exhibit a certain level of technological aptitude in order to be of value in the workplace. Facility with computer and connectivity technology is a set of skills that employers look for in potential employees and that institutes of higher education look for in potential students. A lack of proficiency in these skills can be a bar to entry into either of these areas.

It is no longer enough for driven, economically disadvantaged people to spend hours at either a local or school library, teaching themselves what they need to know in order to succeed. In this age, when library economic resources are generally not even back to the level that they were a generation ago, it is ever more difficult for the economically disadvantaged to make use of what resources there are. Those computers that are put into libraries for public access are generally slow, outdated, and overburdened. Software availability is usually limited, decreasing the utility of those machines that are available to young people trying to increase their chances of success in the Information Age.

The question is not simply one of socioeconomic status, although this is an important contributing factor. Socioeconomic status contributes in the sense that those people of higher status have the resources to give their children a broader view of the world. One way in which this affects a child's outlook is in enhancing a sense of wonder and discovery that leads to an ability to see, and to seize, opportunities. This is more difficult when the model that a child sees is one of working long hours for little reward, while simultaneously being surrounded by images of the "good life" that seem ever out of reach. Understanding the challenges of being engulfed in this environment makes it easier to see how feelings of hopelessness can occur.

The picture is not all gloom and doom. William Rukeyser, coordinator of Learning in the Real World, a non-profit information clearinghouse with a focus on education technology and its effects on children, has reason to believe that economically disadvantaged youth who are able to make a connection with technology resources benefit from the exposure. "A couple of years ago, you very rarely heard evidence or heard opinions questioning the kind of revealed wisdoms that computers were going to help kids learn," he states. "In the last couple of years, we have seen studies by respected publications, respected newspapers, people involved in the field, saying, 'It doesn't appear that there is evidence supporting the notion that computers in all levels of education actually translate into educational performance.' There are some pieces of evidence, certainly anecdotal evidence, that kids who are isolated in one way or another, in fact, do get assistance." Mr. Rukeyser recounts his own experiences with this phenomenon:

> I spent a couple of months on the island of Guam earlier this year. There's a perfect example, kids

thousands of miles away from the nearest urban center, even further from the nearest English-speaking urban center; they don't have access to the kind of information sources that the typical North American kids do in urban and suburban areas. And so when you have got people who are geographically isolated or kids who are isolated by reasons of extreme poverty, or kids who have [other problems] we have got some pretty convincing anecdotal evidence that they are being helped to learn. But just because that is true in those isolated areas, doesn't mean that it's true for all the millions of school kids in America.

And indeed for many school kids in America that isn't true. In 1999, although over half of those school districts that had technical support staff had at least one full-time person, almost one-third of all districts had no one at all. This means that even basic full-time support coverage was available in only about one-third of all schools, a level of support that resulted in less computer access and a less satisfying experience for students. As well, although more computers exist in schools, teacher access remains low, and school assistance in this regard remains noncommittal. In 1998, only in 30 percent of school districts did 75 percent or more of the teachers have computers at home; moreover, district assistance to teachers to purchase computers existed in only slightly over 15 percent of districts. This lack of access to computer resources outside of the educational setting inevitably constrains educators' familiarity and facility with this medium.

More surprisingly, many of the nation's private schools are finding themselves among the digital have-nots. Overall, only half as many of the nation's private schools and classrooms had internet access as did public schools. Additionally, private school educators generally have less training and are paid less than their public school peers, at a time when the employment need for public school teachers with computer skills, as well as the ability to integrate computers and connectivity into the learning curriculum, is expanding. Many of the nation's private schools will have to reexamine their policies and physical capabilities in these areas just to keep up with the public schools.

In light of statistics like these, the digital divide seems even more menacing, and the need to close it even more urgent. Yet there are still caveats to the use of computers and software in the classroom. Ms. Jane Healy, an educator and psychologist with over three decades experience dealing with children's education, and the author of *Failure to Connect: How Computers Affect Our Children's Minds—for Better and Worse*, views with some skepticism the current headlong rush to wire everything, and in so doing completely center education around this new technology. "When you watch kids on computers, you really think they are motivated and we make the assumption from our adult minds that they are motivated to learn," she says. "Of course, why else would they be doing this? Actually I would suggest that what they are motivated to do is use the computer." Ms. Healy believes that, though children may learn as a side effect of using the computer, the computer does not address central issues of a child's development into a healthy, autonomous adult.

She states that "in the motivation research it is very clear that the best way to develop a child who is internally motivated, who will be a self-starter as an adult and won't constantly have someone cracking the whip over them, is to have a child who is internally motivated for achievement. And we call this achievement motivation. External stimuli and external rewards tend to reduce and finally maybe even wipe out this kind of achievement motivation." And external stimuli and rewards are exactly those things the computer is best at providing.

While Healy finds it beneficial for computer technology to be implemented within an age-appropriate educational structure, she believes the current trends may be sending the wrong educational messages to children. "So what you have is a child, then, who comes to the computer, expects a reward [and] then goes into the workplace and expects to get rewarded. . . . Somehow we have got this idea in developing software that the way to make kids want to learn is to make it always fun and to make them always feel successful." In this view, internal motivation to attack a problem for the sheer fun of the challenge is eliminated. One could easily envision the grave consequences for a generation of students ill-equipped to confront, accept, and learn from their failures. What needs to be understood by anyone using software (and especially by educators) is that these programs are not all things to all people. Programmers are human just like the rest of us, with their own visions and vices, allegiances and agendas. The software they create will reflect all of these in some way or other.

Ms. Healy has outlined a strategy for integrating computer and connectivity technology into a well-rounded school program. Hers is a policy of inclusion rather than segregation, creating an atmosphere and environment where all the parts of a curricula are seen to be connected, rather than as compartmentalized units that have no interaction. This in itself fosters a new way of thinking—of seeing a larger picture behind any discrete event—and assists in the growth of critical and analytical thinking. A program with good integration of technology with education will seek out new ways of using that technology to enhance the educational atmosphere. An example might be the use of databases in an English class, a combination that would not be apparent to most English teachers. But through the use of database software, it is possible to graphically show, for instance, that William Shakespeare used roughly twice as many different words in his plays as the average person has in their vocabulary, which could then lead to an investigation of word etymologies from Shakespeare's time to the present.

"I think that good teachers are going to get equal or better results," Healy states of her new plan, "but starting in third, fourth grade, then we can start to look for uses of the applications programs. Maybe the word processing. Perhaps we want to start to teach our children how to do keyboarding. Perhaps we do definitely want to teach them to use spreadsheets and databases because those can be mind expanders in a lot of different ways and can be used to teach almost any subject, really."

WHAT PURPOSE, THEN, DOES COMPUTER and communications technology best serve in the classroom? Is it meant to be a more appealing method of imparting information? Is it meant to be a visual, and virtual, window on the world, showing children the rich diversity of life on our planet, of other cultures and other experiences? Is it meant to be an aid in teaching analytic and problem-solving skills, in educating our youngsters to think for themselves? Is it meant to be a tool to train the next generation of corporate workers?

Ideally, of course, it should be all of these, but the complexities of these issues make the creation of a plan for the integration of computers and communications technology into the classroom far from easy. In addition to the computers themselves, which need a certain level of technological sophistication to actually be anything other than expensive paperweights, a school needs to be physically connected to the internet. The computers also need to have the appropriate software to make that connection usable, and a staff trained to use that software and teach its responsible use to students. Likely, political pressures will require that the computers have one or more of the various filtering protocols in place to monitor and circumscribe access to the internet. All of this—and some of these items are recurring expenses—is just for internet access and use, having nothing to do with applications programs for the computers.

What is more, as the first studies on the effect that technology is actually having on student performance are published, some interesting and perhaps surprising results are surfacing. An on-line newsletter of the National Education Goals Panel cited a study done by the Educational Testing Service last year which professed to offer "the first solid evidence of what works and what doesn't when computers are used in the nation's classrooms." It noted that those fourth and eighth grade students who spent more time on computers actually did *worse* on math tests than those who had less time on the computer. The study also indicated that computer technology is most useful when the educators are well-trained on the integration of the technology into an educational plan.

The wiring of America's public schools and classrooms merely scratches the surface of the digital divide. At the end of the day, the U.S. will have to face a number of issues heretofore ignored, sidetracked, or given only lip service. These issues involve the racial makeup of the U.S. and how we as a people embrace our cultural differences; the vast gulf of socio-economic differences that exist and how we go about bridging it to present truly equal educational opportunities to all the children of our land; and an intense self-scrutiny of our current educational methodologies.

THERE IS CURRENTLY AN AVALANCHE of computer and communications technology being marketed and sold to states, school districts, and private schools around the country. The factors that contribute to this are as diverse as the segments of the post-industrial society in which they are occurring. Scare tactics in the news media and overblown advertising hype create a climate of fear and anxiety about technology. Creating parental anxiety about whether children will be left behind educationally, economically, and, by implication, socially, appears to be as much a part of their intent as any effort to inform. Subsequent parental pressure on schools to buy computers, peripherals, and software contributes to the huge and at times poorly planned expansion in computer and communications services in the schools, usually without much understanding of the computer's best role in the classroom.

The costs of this grand experiment in American education are many, varied, and uncertain. Currently, the federal government has taken a leading role in creating momentum toward the introduction of computers and communications technology into the nation's classrooms. The President proposed a budget for school technology for the year 2000 of $1.5 billion, almost double the budget for 1999. Some of the additional funds would go towards computer training opportunities for educators in U.S. middle schools, a further acknowledgment of the need for adequately trained teachers. As well, the funding for the 21st Century Learning Centers program, designed to provide computer learning opportunities in an after-school setting for close to two hundred thousand children in forty-six states, would be tripled, from $200 to $600 million. This program provides a place for students to use computers in a safe setting during those hours with a statistically high incidence of teenage violence and substance abuse.

Another of the ways in which this massive campaign to wire all public classrooms is being financed is through what is called the "e-rate." Established with bipartisan support in Congress as part of the Telecommunications Act of 1996, the e-rate provides for a 20 to 90 percent discount on telecommunications services, internet access, and internal connections for schools and libraries. Funding for the e-rate program is from long-distance telecommunications provider fees. E-rate funding commitments in 1998 totaled almost $1.7 billion, with about $1.1 billion going to urban schools, $183 million going to rural areas, and the balance to suburban schools. Just over half of the funds will be used to help pay for wiring the schools, and 40 percent will be used to defray the costs of ongoing telecommunications services with the remainder going to related projects. According to FCC documents, thirty-two thousand applicants applied for 1999 e-rate funds, capped at $2.25 billion. Even with funding to the cap, FCC chairman William Kennard indicated that the long-distance telecommunications industry would be receiving over half a billion dollars in reductions and restructuring costs, which he indicated should be used to reduce long-distance rates further.

This program was developed to take advantage of the potential of the internet as an educational tool. It is also supposed to redress some of the growing divide between advantaged and disadvantaged schools and school systems, as funds are targeted at the neediest schools in the nation. This program, in concert with other initiatives, seems to be having some effect. While only a handful of classrooms were wired in 1994, the latest figures indicate that most of the nation's public-school classrooms will soon have regular internet access. In this same period, the percentage of schools (as opposed to individual classrooms) that had internet connections at all grew from 35 percent to 78 percent.

The effect of the e-rate contributions on the availability of communications technology in classrooms is abundantly clear. Although the e-rate fund redresses some of the economic issues surrounding connectivity, other issues still remain. Putting a wire in every classroom, or even a computer on every desk, is merely the physical positioning of an already-existing technology, and in many cases, not even the latest iteration of that technology. The standard model is that the hardware technology changes every year and a half, on average, and those changes are of the "bigger, better, faster, more" variety. Is it reasonable to expect that schools, or the average parents for that matter, will be purchasing new computers every two years? Most schools probably don't even purchase new books with that frequency, and books require a lot less overhead in terms of maintenance, support, and training in their use. This merely supports what most Americans know already: unsupported statements about what we need "right now" should be viewed in a larger context.

At the same time, changes in the perception of the academic environment have allowed businesses, through their salespeople and advertising, greater access to (and perhaps influence in) schools than ever before. On the part of the schools themselves, public and private alike, competition for students, acclaim, and funding all play a part in this feverish push to get wired. At worst, public school systems in the United States are treated as little more than another segment of the consumer economy. Have schools become just another marketing target group to have their buying power appealed to? Are these new technologies serving educators and enabling a better and broader education, or are they seen by the business world as a way to train a better "class" of worker?

There is indeed a current trend in education toward schools entering into "partnerships" with businesses, where an educational institution's focus is almost entirely on workplace preparation. The thrust of education for some schools has become centered on strategies for job procurement, providing students as interns to numerous companies as an unpaid labor force, with minimal attention paid to course work not perceived to have a direct bearing on future employment.

But this may not be the environment that parents want their children in, or the best education for their children to have. The budgetary reallocations that are being made to fund this massive push to give at least the appearance of every classroom's having computer access are being promoted at the expense of other educational programs. This political and budgetary chicanery may in fact be shortchanging many individual groups of students, and curtailing their activities, in an effort to give the appearance that all students are connected. "What is happening, for example, to good remedial reading programs?" asks Jane Healy. "What is happening to our arts programs, which are being cut?... This is the most amazing thing to me, that a country could decide to cut arts and humanities budgets to put in technology for children. We are cutting gym programs. We are cutting library resources. A teacher in one of the Western states said, 'our school system could be IBM as far as the technology is concerned. We have everything. But when I want to get reading books for my kids I can't get the budget approved because it has all been spent on the machines.' Now this is foolish and short-sighted."

To Ms. Healy, one of the roots of the problem is that political considerations and economic pressure are being put before children's welfare. "I think that instead of grandstanding on these budgets, we really need to be thinking seriously, 'How can this help? What kind of funding do we need to put in to develop the right kinds of software?' To develop the research that is going to tell us how to use this effectively before we keep just flooding machines into the schools that are, in most case, frankly being misused."

Given a choice, then, parents certainly need to examine whether cutting programs to put in technology which does not have a demonstrated and documented effectiveness in learning and may, in fact, have a negative effect on children's long-term development, is worth the short-term peace of mind brought by blindly believing that this technology is "the answer." Not that computers don't have an important place in education. As Ms. Healy states, "In good schools, where this is being done well, this [bad allocation] is not happening, because the computers are being used as an adjunct to a very rich, full program. And that is what we might hope that all our children would have an opportunity to experience."

Good schools, of course, start with good teachers, and there are many educators in the United States who have embraced the new computer and communications technologies. Kristi Rennebohm Franz is representative of the educators with whom we hope that our children will come in contact, one of the "next-generation" teachers as comfortable with a keyboard as with a stick of chalk.

Since 1994, Ms. Rennebohm Franz has been a lead teacher with the International Educational and Resource Network (I*EARN), through which she coordinated the Global Art and Water Habitats projects. Her classroom research focuses on literacy and telecommunications, and she is involved in leadership collaborations for educational technology regionally, nationally, and internationally. "The Global Art Project connects visual arts in a wonderful way and shows the different visual art tools that people have in different countries," she

said. "The batiks of Thailand, the different ways that the in-
digenous people in the Zuni pueblo in New Mexico create their
art work and the tools that they use to do that. Children can
see the richness of the tapestry of cultures that we have in our
world through children's art."

The Global Art Project—part of a growing trend called "electronic field trips"—works as a collaborative effort, motivated by
a diverse group of educators around the country. These educators and their classes are in contact through the internet.
One might suggest a group art project revolving around folk
tales from around the world. Other educators and their students respond to the proposed project until a group of ten to
twelve classes are involved. Students in each of these classes
then create an original work of art based on the theme of a folk
tale, coupled with an original piece of writing.

After the creative process is finished, some of the artwork is
retained at the school that created it and some of it is sent on—
by mail, as a graphic file over the internet, or even posted to a
website for downloading—to each of the other schools in the
group. In this manner, not only are young students exposed to
a variety of educational experiences in their own classroom,
but they get to share those experiences with others in sometimes distant places, and gain from the experiences of other
students and contact with different segments of their own culture or perhaps even other cultures.

Ms. Rennebohm Franz's project, as an integrated form of
educating, covers several subject areas and makes the entire
experience more meaningful than simply looking at pictures in
a book and pointing out a place on a map. "The Global Art Project emphasized the arts, it emphasized the social studies, the

multiculturalism of our cultures through the arts and through language, and the multilingual dimensions of our globe," she said. "There's no piece of the curriculum that can't be pulled into it, because you're working with communicating between real people and real places around the world. It's not virtual—it's real."

Critics of these initiatives—and of the introduction of computer and communications technology into educational settings in general—take issue more with the particulars of the presentation than with the information presented. "When I feel the difference between what it means to be playing games, creativity—ideas are bouncing off," said Douglas Goodkin, a music educator at a San Francisco school. "And when I compare that to what it's like to step into a computer lab, I see that all these intelligences are being missed. There isn't a physical involvement, there's not a sensorial involvement, there's not a human social involvement. There's not much." Ms. Rennebohm Franz's experience, however, has been very different: "We discovered very quickly that the opportunity for them [students] to talk to each other—and that's how they describe it—on-line through their written text was providing them incredible motivation to work hard on the writing skills that we were doing in the classroom," she said. "It gave them an extra incentive and motivation to do that when they realized that their writing was going to an audience that they knew. These are all important parts of the writing process."

While there is little debate over the value of the multiculturalism inherent in these projects, there is a feeling among some academics that computers and communications technology introduces a "gee-whiz" aspect to learning that is counterproductive. However, at a time when these same aspects of television, films, and video games make interaction with a visual interface more appealing, and traditional methods of schooling even less of interest to many children, one might think that schools need all the gee-whiz they can get.

IN MARCH OF 1999, PRESIDENT Clinton reaffirmed his administration's commitment to making the benefits of the digital future available to all of the nation's schoolchildren. In his remarks, he said, "Computers, the internet, and educational software can make a real difference in the way teachers teach and students learn. Because of our efforts, children in the most isolated inner city or rural town will have access to the same universe of knowledge as a child in the most affluent suburb. Parents will be able to communicate more frequently with teachers, and keep up with the progress of their child in school. Our children will be 'technologically literate,' and better prepared for the high-tech, high-wage jobs of the future."

Should these predictions come about, through both the equal distribution and installation of hardware and the across-the-board application of knowledge to use these technologies to enhance the educational experience, all of our children can become "technologically literate," and live richer lives as well as be better prepared to enter the workforce of the Information Age. But educational computer and communications technology is still in its infancy and money is being made available without any organized determination as to what to spend it on and whether it should be spent at all on any particular "initiative." As William Rukeyser has said, "In these early years of education technology, it's been the idea, 'Hey we can get a little bit of extra money, maybe we can write a grant and get some money from a foundation, or a company, or from the state or federal government.' And so essentially, this equipment will come in and it will be no cost to us." This reasoning process has likely led to the downfall of a good many well-intentioned initiatives. "What they don't stop to realize," Mr. Rukeyser continues, "is that when you've got what is referred to as the 'boxes and wires' installed in the school, that is just the beginning. You have only begun to pay at that point, so even if you have gotten 80 to 90 percent of the installation taken care of for you, there is still, for an average-size school district, maybe millions, maybe tens of millions of dollars to keep paying out." And not once, but year after year.

Many school districts get into financial difficulties right from the beginning. Mr. Rukeyser cites one study done on the magnitude of the situation. "The Mackenzie Company, which is a consulting firm in Washington, did a study for the White House, and it estimated that each and every year after computers have been installed in the school, that school district should be prepared to pay at least one-third of the purchase cost, the initial cost, for such things as training, replacement, repairs, upgrades." What this means to an average school district is that, for every one million dollars laid out for initial computer and communications infrastructure purchases, it is going to cost about $350,000 every year thereafter to stay up and running with relatively current equipment and training.

For example, within the last year, the Kentucky State Education Department has been ordered to purchase filtering software for all of its almost twenty-four hundred schools, district offices, and department of education members. This software is intended to capture the locations of educationally desirable websites, and block access to undesirable ones. One of the positive side effects is expected to be that the current 56k internet connections will perform at the same level as T1 lines, since all desktop operations will now go through the servers with the filters. If each school was intended to have a T1 line, this would save each school five to six thousand dollars per year, at an initial cost of only $200,000. Little has been mentioned about upgrades or maintenance costs, or the cost of training. Additionally, there are the potential costs to provide the same software and training to the state's libraries, where children would be able to access the same information as in the schools.

The inability of most schools to accumulate and apply cash reserves of this size for a single program on an annual basis will inevitably lead to a diminishment of the utility of those computers and their infrastructure, which represent perhaps tens of billions of dollars in investment nationwide. However, with the proper planning, training, and the appropriate use of our technological and human resources, the twenty-first century will fulfill the promise of these technologies with benefits that enrich the lives of all of our nation's citizens, not just those who can easily afford the entry fees.

2

The Future
of Work

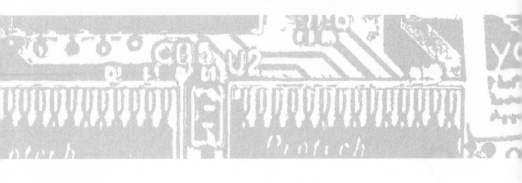

The nature of employment in the United States is in the grip of fundamental change. The flight of manufacturing jobs to nations where the cost of manual labor is cheaper and production costs are less expensive due to lower levels of government safety and environmental regulation have changed the vocational landscape. Industry consolidation and automation have eliminated large numbers of jobs in many sectors, and the large-scale introduction of computers into the workplace has changed the very nature of many jobs from hands-on to computer-aided or controlled processes requiring an entirely different skill set. In this transition from the Industrial Age to the Information Age, manufacturing jobs, once the golden gateway to the middle class for many of the economically disadvantaged, are giving way to lower-paying service jobs. It is becoming increasingly clear that if you're not one of the digiterati, your career prospects will be worrisome.

This change in the nature of employment brings with it the need for a change in the focus of education. In order to succeed in the new economy, learning has to be not only a means to an end, but an end in itself. As Robert Reich has explained it, education is not just "learning passively, it's not just sitting back and acquiring facts, it's learning interactively, it's feeling and understanding how to be empowered to gain additional knowledge. And that in fact is what the technological revolution is all about.... It's not just education and skills we are talking about, we are talking about the ability to think quickly on the job. It's not as if you have an advantage just because you have a lot of facts at your disposal. What you need to do is be able to learn quickly. What you need to do is to figure out in any situation what you need to know, and get the information you need, analyze that information."

Education and employment have become more intimately entwined than ever before and access to technology is not only necessary to round out a student's education, but is also crucial in making that student eligible for future employment. At the most basic level, public high schools now have the dual responsibilities of teaching students to be well-rounded citizens and introducing them to the basic skills needed to succeed in the workplace. Yet while everyone agrees that computer and communications technology and training are a necessary part of education going into the twenty-first century, there is little agreement on when, how, or the extent to which they should be used in the educational context.

Given the complex hierarchical structure of the administration of secondary education, it's easy to see why. Federal involvement in determining educational requirements is usually of an advisory nature, giving the individual states information from which to build a curriculum, forecast social needs, or coordinate national initiatives, based on factors deemed important to the nation. The federal government also has a mandate to ensure that all citizens' civil rights are protected in the school environment. It can, if necessary, wield the implicit threat of withholding economic contributions to the schools. Additionally, there are a number of national organizations serving the interests of educators and specific subject areas that also contribute ideas and voice their concerns about education. (Examples of these include the National Institute for Science Education, the National Education Institute, and the American Federation of Teachers.)

The state government is generally where the concrete conditions for the fulfillment of secondary-school graduation requirements are decided. Many of the state departments of education are charged with determining the depth and breadth of subject coverage and the means of assessing student facility with the subject material. This is done for a range of subjects from the social to the physical sciences, from foreign languages to computer languages. As on the national level, there are numerous state-wide organizations representing the concerns of educators and administrators. The district level is where federal and state guidelines and legislation are coordinated and implemented in the individual public secondary schools.

With so many players in the education game, it would seem impossible to achieve consensus. However, this much remains certain: with educational needs still being met primarily with local tax assessments, inner cities, rural regions, and other economically disadvantaged areas will continue to trail well-off communities and the suburbs. This will be the case in their ability to access newer technology, to maintain their existing technology and infrastructure, and to train educators in the use and teaching of computer and communications technology. What we are talking about here is not schools that have computers that are three or more years old, with software that is a generation (usually two years) out of date. We are talking about schools in areas with such a depressed tax base that they worry about having sufficient resources to heat the schools in winter, to have enough books for each student, or to keep the ceilings from leaking when it rains. These are the schools at most risk of being stranded across the digital divide.

Yet there is another, newer player directly involved in schools at the end of the twentieth century, one that may prove most helpful in crossing the divide, though again at a cost: American business. While the relationship of public education and business has generally been one of arms-length interaction, second only to the separation of church and state in the minds of many educators, this is in the process of change.

MANY FIRMS REALIZE BENEFITS BY being involved in the educational setting, for a variety of reasons. Some work with schools to provide an environment where students can acquire the skills necessary to fill positions in areas that currently have a lack of candidates. Some follow a more materialistic aim in getting "their" equipment, software, or training program accepted into schools in order to "build name recognition and brand loyalty" as it might be stated in the language of marketing. As in any other area, motivations run the gamut from altruism to pecuniary gain.

The partnering of schools and business can take many forms. One model is that of Travis High School in Austin,

Texas. In an effort to battle the small percentage of students going on to post-secondary education and a troubled history that included gang activity, the high school partnered with local technology companies to open a Communications Academy as a part of the school. The Travis Communications Academy is a school-to-career institution developed to allow students to specialize in the areas of multimedia, teleproduction, and telecommunications. Students learn about the processes and software in their chosen area of study, enhancing their chances of employment in these fields or continuing their education at college or university. The availability of this program has proven to be a source of insight and hope for some students. One of the students, Louisa Segura-Robles, is a case in point. When she first entered the school, she spent much of her time hanging out with friends who were "kind of involved with gangs." The Communications Academy opened up a new world to her. She realized "This gang life ain't for me . . . computers have changed my life so many ways. When I got into the multimedia class my sophomore year, that first year is when I had changed, you know, I got out of the gang. If it wasn't for computers, I might even be dead." That same year, Louisa got her first job. After saving for three years, she was able to buy a computer of her own. She also began an internship at a local elementary school working with third- through fifth-grade children, teaching them the same skills, and hopefully lessons, that she learned.

Another example can be seen at New Technology High School in American Canyon, California. Known as the "school that business built," New Tech High boasts 250 computers for 220 students and a significant involvement in the school on the part of the local high-tech business community. In fact, the school's set-up is a direct response to the needs of local business. As the school's director, Mark Morrison, describes the relationship, business leaders approached the community and said "You know, your graduates aren't fulfilling our employment needs.... They're not reading, writing, computing well enough, and they certainly don't have the technological expertise to help us grow a technological economic cluster in the Napa Valley." Hence, schools like New Technology High focus on computer and business skills, and the business influence is everywhere. For example, Mark Morrison points out that the color schemes in the school came directly from Silicon Graphics. "You can kinda see they left their footprint all over the building," he said.

The new student at New Technology High is someone like Travis Eliason. Travis had been enamored of computers since he was young, playing on his aunt's computer. Although he did not own his own computer until he was a teenager, his mother hoped that he could "use his brains and go somewhere with it." In making the decision to shift from his former high school, Vintage High in American Canyon, to New Technology High, Travis left both friends and traditional education behind. While he stays in touch with his friends from Vintage High, the differences in their attitudes about computers, as well as in their levels of skill, have widened the gulf between Travis and his friends over time. As Travis says, "They're kind of overwhelmed. When they came to my school one day, they seen all the computers and they're, like, 'Man, you're, like, some kind of genius, aren't you?' And I was, like, no, I mean, it's just computers. You can't be afraid of them."

Travis is grateful for the opportunity that has been provided to him at New Tech High. He sees that his friends at Vintage High look at computers in a very different way than he does now. Trying to examine the differences between them, Travis said, "They don't want to interact with them [computers], like on e-mail or on-line, with other people in chat rooms. They kind of just want to get out of high school, and they really don't have, like, basically, like, a real structure [of] what they want to do afterwards." He feels that being at New Tech High has given him more structure, and forced him to look at schooling and the future in a more realistic light. "When I came to New Tech, it [a plan] was kind of enforced, you know, 'you're going to need a plan.' I mean, this is the real world. You gotta go out and do something."

A third scenario is that of Monta Vista High School in Cupertino, California. Monta Vista was one of the first high schools in the nation to be connected to the internet, and as such gained national attention when Vice President Al Gore visited in 1994. The principal of Monta Vista High, Mary Stone, talked a little about the benefits of being an educational institution in the heart of Silicon Valley. "We have a lot of donations of equipment that come from computer companies. We have parents who are CEOs of computer companies, and they make available to us special staff development that's extremely beneficial to our teachers."

Sidra Durst, a student at Monta Vista, has grown up with computers; her father works with computers and they have four of them at home. Sidra believes that she has benefited in a number of ways from being a part of the Silicon Valley community. She feels that in going to a school supported by the Silicon Valley, "it's almost assumed that you're going to go into a career related to computers and technology, simply because all the resources are here. That's what the focus of education is on." Sidra is exposed to the tools of new technology every day, as well as being in an atmosphere where the educators and other students are comfortable interacting in the language of this technology. She knows that she is being trained to work, and lead, in the new economy. "I've just been so comfortable using expensive and highly advanced technology," she said, "that I know when I get into college or when I'm in the workforce, I'll be able to just work with it really easily."

Like Louisa at Travis High, Sidra also makes it a point to pass on the knowledge she has acquired. Sidra volunteers at a Community Technology Center where she assists low-income youth with learning computer skills. This passing on of knowledge, expertise, and values is one of the most positive aspects of the technological revolution, and is greatly helping to reduce the alienation and anxiety that keeps people in low-income communities away from technology. Sidra believes that more should be done by business and government to help people across the divide. "They are overlooking the digital divide," she said, "and I think for people that haven't even gotten a basic foothold on it, now it's going to be difficult to jump in and catch up with everyone else."

IN ADDITION TO BRINGING TECHNOLOGY and computer education into the schools themselves, some businesses are also assisting schools by providing direct job experience to students prior to graduation. In the past, students were introduced to different professions in many ways, by having community professionals and parents visit the school to talk about their jobs, or having students go into the workplace for a day. As they reached high school, the students might also partake in career days at school, where they could talk to representatives from different companies and other employment resources. Many students in high school also held part-time jobs in the community, to have responsibility, their own money, or to save for college. Today, though, there is a new way: the School-to-Work Movement. Its avowed goal is to give children experience with work at an early age through structured job internships. Not work in a fast-food outlet, but work in offices and hospitals, doing the same type of technical jobs that are listed in classified ads in the newspaper.

Those who champion the School-to-Work movement believe that this type of program addresses the needs of both those students who are going on to post-secondary education and those who are going directly into the workforce. Hilary Pennington, President of Jobs for the Future, stated that "in the good programs, there is attention to having there be a workplace mentor, to having a learning plan for what skills the young person should be gaining as a result of that work experience. Young people have the opportunity to do exhibitions and performances that show that they have gained progressive mastery of more complex work." These are indeed valuable skills for both the business and education environment.

Critics of the School-to-Work movement point to the fact that American businesses now expect high schools to take on the burden of on-the-job training or provide apprenticeships that historically have been a part of the American business structure. At the same time, businesses want schools to provide students during business hours, which are the same as the school day. Some even see the partnership as little more than a ploy for free labor under the guise of internships. As noted by the CEO Forum on Education and Technology in Washington, schools currently spend about eighty-eight dollars per student on computer equipment, while spending a mere six dollars per student on training educators how to use and teach students the use of the more sophisticated applications programs. This averages out to about one course per year for educators to learn how to use this technology, without assistance from the business community.

Another concern is whether partnerships like these will give business an inordinate amount of influence over what is actually taught in the affected schools. In its most extreme form, the movement could also be seen as precipitating a two-tiered system of secondary education, where some students go to high schools geared toward college admission, and others go to schools with a vocational emphasis. For instance, one organization that is already involved in studying the integration of work and school is the Committee for Economic Development, a non-profit organization comprised primarily of U.S. business leaders and corporate heads. Their Subcommittee on the Employer's role in Linking School and Work is composed of forty-nine individuals, nine of whom are identified as officials at universities (18 percent) and only one of whom is identified as having any direct connection to education below the university level at all (2 percent). The majority of the rest of the subcommittee is composed of chairmen and presidents of American corporations. In situations like these, when the business end of the partnership is so predominant, some fear that non-business segments of the curriculum like music and the arts, or even extra-curricular activities, may not receive the support they deserve.

However, at its best, in a balanced educational setting, the School-to-Work movement may provide one of the few real opportunities available to rural or economically disadvantaged educational institutions. "One of the most promising movements in helping prepare young people for success in this new economy is the School-to-Work movement," said Hilary Pennington. "Particularly [for] young people in inner city neighborhoods, it gives them access to a whole new group of adults who begin to care about them . . . counsel them and help them, in fact, move on to college." Ms. Pennington sees business partnerships as the future of American education, with students and educators "figuring out, together with business and community partners, how to give kids greater experience with work. Not just exposure, but experience."

IN THE END, THE JURY IS STILL OUT over the success, or even merit, of the School-to-Work movement. Educators such as Jane Healy express their concern about the school environments that are created by such close links with the business community. "Schools are not training grounds, or should not be training grounds, for a corporate workforce," she said. "Their purpose is much different. Schools should not be about making a living, but about making a life." Advocates like Hilary Pennington, however, feel that a life—or more specifically, a chance at a better life—is exactly what the movement provides. "It's giving them opportunities to enter more structured apprenticeships, where they really are part of an adult team, and we are finding that many, many young people, teenagers, find this a way that makes their school learning come alive for them," she said.

Of the students mentioned here, all of whom were in special technology-related programs, and most of whom were involved in internships, only Sidra Durst went on to college immediately after high school. Travis Eliason graduated, but was unable to go directly to college. Louisa Segura-Robles, weighed down by having to have a paying job after school as well as her internship and other technology-related activities, was not able to graduate with her class, but she did graduate recently.

IN STATING THAT THE DIGITAL DIVIDE is not just a technology problem, we are trying to present the whole panoply of social and economic issues that also contribute to it. If children have grown up in an environment where education is valued, it is easier to draw them in to participate in new educational experiences such as computer classes, because their background has prepared them to accept new experiences. If children grow up in an environment where they don't see education as a path out of their straitened circumstances, it will be that much more difficult to get them to buy into computer literacy as a way of improving their futures. In such a case, new initiatives must be tried, new ways of thinking, as the business buzz phrase goes, "outside the box."

Some departments in the federal government are taking into account this broader view of the digital divide and trying to narrow the gap. Under the leadership of both former Assistant Secretary of Commerce Larry Irving and the current Assistant Secretary of the Department of Commerce, the National Telecommunications and Information Administration (NTIA) has been influential in keeping those who are in isolated areas or economically underprivileged in the public consciousness. In addition to trying to assist in making the nation and its businesses ready to enter the twenty-first century through initiatives in telecommunications and information technology, the NTIA has attempted to implement policies that reflect the broad diversity and multiple needs of all segments of the U.S. population. "We've also been trying to put programs in place out in, really, the bread basket of America," Mr. Irving stated, "in the communities and Native American reservations; inner city communities; low-income districts; rural America. [We want to] make sure that people who have not been part of the Information Age, [the] Information Economy, get prepared. . . . What we're trying to do is get technology where the kids really are. And then [for them to] learn that technology is not just for nerds. It's not just for geeks. It's about them, too."

However, it will take much work on the part of all of us in order to prevent segments of our population from remaining stranded on the far side of the digital divide. In order to accomplish this, of course, access to tools and training is necessary. Just as necessary, however, is appropriate education about the place in U.S. business that these tools now occupy, both for those already in the workforce and for students who will be joining the New Economy. Without an understanding of the role technology will play in their jobs and lives, many people will not be able to understand why they need these skills.

The previous section addressed the different ways in which American business has partnered with schools, which ideally would provide students with both technology and an understanding of its larger context. Aside from their exposure to computer technology in the schools, young people can also get involved with computers outside of the classroom. This is not the equivalent of going off by yourself with a book to improve your mind. There are technical skills, team skills, and a specialized vocabulary to master as well. It is also not, typically, a skill set that many economically disadvantaged parents can help their children attain by demonstrating at home. In many cases, even if one does have the self-motivation to bootstrap oneself across the digital divide, multimedia-capable computers, modems, connectivity software, internet accounts, and other necessary paraphernalia remain out of financial reach. The same economic constraint is present in the ability of these families to purchase either software or self-teaching books to learn to use software, neither of which is inexpensive.

Outside of home and school, there are admittedly few resources available for young people to learn these skills. Although more libraries are recognizing the need to be community resources for computer education, and some are very forward-thinking in terms of offering basic classes in on-line research and computer use, many others still offer nothing more than computerized cataloging, if that. To many, libraries are still thought of primarily as repositories for print materials, institutions that need to divide up their already limited budgets between maintenance of listings, new print materials, and possibly other materials such as audio or video recordings and equipment. The expense of technology and computer resources put additional strain on library budgets, one result of which is a limited number of available terminals and internet connections, leading to long lines and crippling time limitations on patrons' use.

Luckily, there is some acknowledgment that there needs to be more community support for learning the whole palette of skills necessary for success in the Information Age. This is where organizations like Plugged In can be of great assistance to a community. Founded in 1992, Plugged In is a community technology center (CTC) located in East Palo Alto, California. Its goal is to ensure that all residents can take advantage of the opportunities presented by the digital revolution. Such organizations, receiving initial funding from a variety of sources, can look at a community's overall needs and develop a program to address them. "We spend a lot of time trying to figure out how can we build a series of programs that are going to effectively use technology, to make the technology available to everyone in East Palo Alto, not just kids or teens or adults," said Bart Decrem, one of the directors of Plugged In. "But [we] really try to look at the entire community and how we can make the technology available."

Plugged In currently serves a variety of community needs. It has programs geared towards developing different skills for different age groups. There is Plugged In Greenhouse, an innovative after-school program for children, mixing arts and crafts with learning creative computer skills. They have also pioneered a teen enterprises program, wherein a group of teenagers has actually started a business called Plugged In Enterprises, to build web pages and take on desktop publishing jobs for Silicon Valley customers—yet another example of combining education with real-life experience. Plugged In also runs a Technology Access Center, used by both teenagers and adults. At this center, Mr. Decrem notes, "people can come in and use computers and the internet to look for a job, build their small businesses, do their homework, or get ahead in life and use the technology as a tool to accomplish that."

The innovation that seems most indicative of Plugged In's goals, though, is the concept of a community cooperative. The Center is not a free resource, with users having to pay a nominal fee. But they are also told that they may volunteer to help others in lieu of fees, and many people do. This strengthens the community ties, and gives everyone a vested interest in the success of Plugged In. People help in any way they can, cleaning, painting, and even training new users. Mr. Decrem believes this to be an important aspect of ensuring the success of the project. "We're looking at how to engage community members. Instead of saying this is a program that we're offering to the community, let's think of this as a community collaborative that we're making happen together. I think as we start pursuing these kinds of models, then our work starts becoming more sustainable."

Mr. Decrem sees a need for making learning relevant to students who come from environments where learning does not get a lot of support, or gets prioritized downward in the day-to-day scramble of trying to make ends meet. A spiral of declining grades and declining interest in education and learning can result. This, combined with other problems in the home, community, or school can lead to increased drop-out rates and further social alienation. Plugged In tries to give those students the life skills necessary to go on and successfully learn technical skills. It also provides an environment for building self-esteem, gaining a sense of accomplishment and purpose, and creating ties in the community. "What's so powerful to me about what we're doing at Plugged In Enterprises is that the learning is relevant and makes sense," Mr. Decrem said. "We're working with a very small group of students, right here in the neighborhood. We have somebody from the community who's doing the work with the kids. And when they do something, there's kind of an ecosystem that makes sense. It's kind of like you do the work, if you treat the customer right, at the end of the day you get paid."

At Plugged In, and other community technology centers like it, young people marketing their expertise to local businesses must encompass a wider world rather than simply using their skills and computer knowledge. "Then the teens understand why it's important to dress professionally or to be able to write properly or to be able to do things that are perfect and that are not sloppy," Mr. Decrem explains. "Because they see why that's important, and everything becomes relevant. So that the learning takes on meaning." This prepares the teens for future success in the digital work place.

If programs such as Plugged In are to be a necessary adjunct to whatever vocational training may be available through public education, then some thought also needs to be given to constructing the business plans for these programs so that they will be around for the long haul. The challenge for nonprofit organizations and social-change programs is to find a way of creating a sustainable economic future for themselves so that they can continue to provide the necessary services to the community. Although government funding such as that provided by the Department of Commerce's program, which has incubated and helped along groups like Plugged In, is very helpful in setting up resources to those in need, it would be imprudent to rely on continuous government funding. There are other models to look at; for instance, a funding base secured from regular revenues from the telecommunications industry, in the same manner as public access television is funded through cable revenues. However, given that a program as simple as the current e-rate funding for connectivity items like internet access is already coming under fire at the beginning of its second year, it seems unlikely that any other such programs would make it past politicians and into legislation.

Programs like Plugged In also need to respond to new technological challenges in the future, so that those served in the community do not find themselves falling further and further behind until they are shut out of the opportunities of the future. The most successful ones, like Mr. Decrem's, are finding that serving the community can mean good business. "At Plugged In, the way we're addressing that is trying to really make sure that every dollar we spend is spent in the most effective way possible," he said. "The beauty of what we're doing at Plugged In Enterprises is that slowly it's becoming self-sustaining. So in a couple of years that program might actually be able to sustain itself through the revenues that it earns from its corporate customers."

Education in the Information Age that simply follows the standard formula of using a mass-production technique of teaching will inevitably fail many students. And this will mean that the lack of necessary skills for success in the digital workplace will leave those without these skills stranded on the far side of an increasingly huge divide. It is therefore heartening to see that non-profit organizations, as well as the various levels of government, are beginning to look at these other issues that affect many high-school-aged youths, and are implementing non-traditional methods of bringing this technology and training to them. "If we don't make that investment, what are we doing to those kids?" asks Larry Irving. "Are we going to do the right thing for our children? Or are we just going to continue to watch them not have the skills they need to exist in this new society, and watch the divide get wider and wider?"

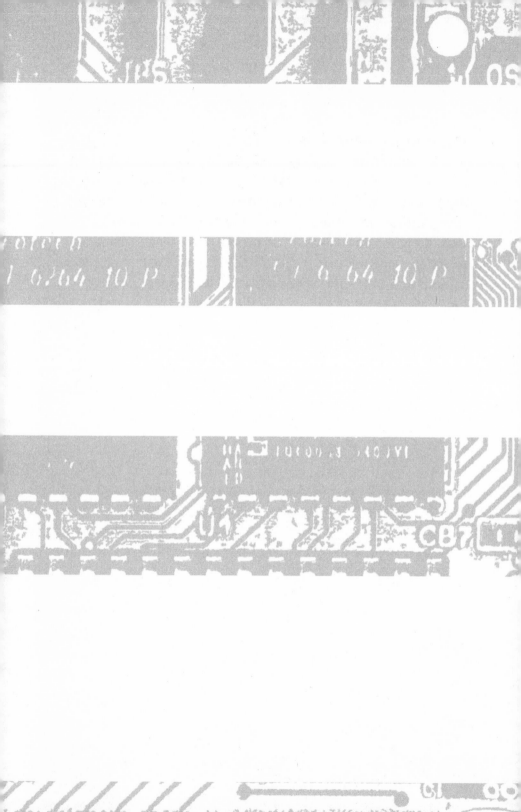

3

The Gender Gap

As we enter an era where good employment opportunities rely on good computer skills, the digital divide takes on increasing social ramifications. The division between the digital haves and have-nots is not only one of economic status, but splits along social lines, as well. At a time when women are becoming more and more of a presence in the American workforce, they also run a greater risk of being shut out of the digital future. Part of the problem is the computer technology industry, a field in which men vastly outnumber women. However, the problem also exists in the schools themselves, in the ways that girls are taught to understand—or not understand—the role of technology in their lives. It took specific legislation to ensure that young women could have equal access to coaches, fields, and sports equipment in school. The access to technology and training for girls is no less important and the limits on it no less pronounced. In fact, girls may be at a technological disadvantage long before they ever graduate from high school and enter the job market.

This gap within the divide is a gender gap between those who are willing to see technology as gender-neutral and those who are not, and it is a specific example of a more common classroom phenomenon. In many schools, educators regularly (albeit sometimes unknowingly) accede to prevailing cultural imperatives and focus more of their attention on male class members, sending a message to the girls that they are not as important. This also sends a message to the boys in the classroom that their "natural" position is superior, and that they will both be praised and challenged more than their female classmates. Add to this the various social pressures that cause many girls to lose confidence in their own abilities once they enter the maelstrom of middle school. "Girls typically undervalue their ability level," Jo Sanders, Director of the Center for Gender Equity at Washington Research Institute, explains. "If a girl gets a B, she will say 'Well, that's not very good.' Or sometimes a girl will get an A and say, 'Well, yeah, I got an A, but I just memorized it. I really don't understand it.' Whereas boys typically overvalue their ability level. If a boy gets a C or a D, he'll say, 'That's okay. I really understood it. I know I did.'" In a case like this, the higher-achieving girl may well eventually lose interest in her studies, a type of self-imposed censure that can have long-lasting consequences.

The Center for Gender Equity has been doing studies on gender perception since 1982. When boys in one of these studies were asked how their lives would be different if they woke up one morning and found that they were girls, their answers were mostly framed in negative terms. When girls were asked what their lives would be like if they suddenly became boys, the answers overwhelmingly indicated that they felt they would have more options and less fears than presently. "[T]he answers are rather heartbreaking, actually," Ms. Sanders said. "The theme of their answers is that the boys envision femininity as constraints, as limitation, as the girls envision masculinity as freedom and liberation." And the answers have not changed since 1982.

The experience of Vickie N. Dunlevy, a seventh-grade science teacher at Fulmore Middle School in Austin, Texas, confirms this view. "In the seventh grade, studies have found that girls typically drop back," she said. "They might have excelled in science and math forever, you know, first grade on, kindergarten on. But around this age, puberty, around twelve years old, thirteen, for whatever reason, if it's because they don't want to seem smart or they don't want to seem aggressive or pushy, the girls tend to step back." As to why all of these influences affect girls this way, while boys appear to remain less affected in their performance, it is likely that a variety of social circumstances are at work. The extra attention in class that boys garner from teachers, the underlying expectations of future social roles, and peer pressures all play a part in psychological reactions that cause girls to lose confidence in their ability to do as well as boys. Fulmore is in many ways like schools around the nation. Situated in the "Silicon Valley" of the Southwest, Austin's Fulmore Middle School started in 1886 as a one-room schoolhouse. Today, it has a student population of over nine hundred. Former Governor Ann Richards taught at Fulmore. The school has received a grant from Microsoft founder Bill Gates, and is at the center of numerous education and technology initiatives. Many of Fulmore's female students are affected by the technological gender gap. But, as we shall see, individual and collective efforts are being made there and around the country to help bring girls into the digital future.

PREFERENTIAL TREATMENT OF BOYS in the classroom naturally extends to the teaching of technology. As noted earlier, very few of the nation's schools have enough reliable, up-to-date computers for every student in a regular class to have their own. With numerous students at one computer at any time, the activities surrounding operating the computer are divided among the students at the computer. In many classrooms, as in life outside of school, boys jockey to be the first in line. There is a perception among the male students that it is acceptable for boys to not follow instructions, to not take turns, and to monopolize the educator's attention, all to the detriment of the rest of the students. "What you see when you go into a classroom is that there tends to be a few boys, not all boys, but a few boys who get the lion's share of the teacher's attention," said Peggy Orenstein, author of *School Girls: Young Women, Self-Esteem and the Confidence Gap.* "And they have a tendency to yell out, to not pay attention to the rules."

Jennifer Cantu talks about what it is like being in such a class environment at Fulmore: "They [boys] tend to talk more than listen in class. It messes up your thinking. Because you're concentrating on one thing and then they start talking, and then they just mess you up because you're used to, like, a pattern of how you are thinking. And then when they talk, it breaks the pattern and you have to start all over." In such an environment, many girls, even those who earlier showed an aptitude for computers and technology, begin to show less and less of an interest in computers. "When you have a computer [in class]," explained Sarah Schulman, a thirteen-year-old at Fulmore, "I think girls are frightened by how much the guys go to the mouse, and so they step back and they let the males dominate the computer." This sense of restraint on the part of girls cannot but affect their ability to excel in an academic setting.

What is more, girls and boys approach the very use of computers in different ways. Boys tend to just hop on and poke around, to see what the computer can and cannot do, testing the limits of both the technology and themselves. In general, the computer is seen as more of a toy than a tool. On the other hand, girls tend to view computer technology with specific uses in mind, and want to know what it is they need to do in order to achieve their purpose in using the equipment. This makes using computer technology more difficult, because they need to have both a familiarity with the equipment and instruction in how to achieve their goals before they ever set finger to keyboard for a specific purpose. "Girls often tend to make their use of computers contingent upon what they need the computer to do," explained Jo Sanders, "while boys will often be very happy to sit there and simply mess with it, just to see what will happen when they mess with it." Software developer Janese Swanson confirms this view. "Girls play in a different way than boys do with the computer," she said. "Girls have the same zeal for using technology and feel the same joy and passion in playing with the technology. But girls—and I'm going to go for the stereotyping here, from the research—girls tend to like depth and the connection to people and information that helps them in their lives. And that's part of their play."

This also leads to a sense of trepidation when they approach anything mechanical or electronic that is unfamiliar. "When I first used the computer I think I was frightened by it because I felt, 'What happens if I press this button?,'" said Sarah Schulman. "'Would that be wrong and would I mess up something that was so expensive?' I think just being afraid is your biggest obstacle and once you overcome that, you can do almost everything." This means that, if girls are to be given the same opportunities as boys to use computers and gain the skills necessary to succeed in the digital workplace, then they need to be trained to have the courage to confront the technology and master it on their terms, even if that means failing at first. "One of the best things that you can do for your daughter is to let her fall flat on her face," notes Peggy Orenstein. "So when you see a girl who messes up, you have to let her do that. You have to let her try it again and try it again until she gets it right. Because that is the only way that girls work through their fear of failure."

Hence we need to come to a fuller understanding of the ways in which girls are taught, or not taught, to live and work in the Information Age, and we need to provide the tools and training for them to be full partners in the future now rushing towards us. This is not always easy, as it is difficult to take ourselves outside of our usual acculturation and reach that fuller perspective. "Parents in particular, you know, we love our kids, we don't want to raise our daughters and our sons differently," explained Ms. Orenstein. "But we grew up in this culture too and so often the messages we give our kids, whether it's about appearance or about kind of acting out behavior, physicality—

we don't mean to give our daughters and our sons different kinds of feedback, but we do."

As adolescents search for a way to fit in, a way to be socially accepted, it is easy for them to adopt roles that they see as being traditionally acceptable. And even in the face of the obvious, many trained educators will see what they *expect* to see, rather than the actual state of affairs in the classroom. "A lot of times, I'd walk into a classroom where computers were being used and the teacher would say, 'The girls are using the computers. Everybody is using the computers,'" explained Ms. Orenstein. "And then I'd walk up and look at a lab group, and you listen to what they were doing, watch what they were doing, and you'd realize the kids had fallen into very gender-specific roles."

Additionally, she continues, girls are given a set of socialized behaviors that do not lend themselves to success in achieving confidence and independence:

> From the time that they are little, girls look for their validation much more outside of themselves than boys do. Everything from "You are so cute, you are so pretty," to being good, to toeing the line, to following the rules, girls are always looking outside.... Boys tend to find the locus of their self-esteem much more from within. And so as they get older, girls develop more of a fear of humiliation, more of a fear of looking stupid in front of other people, more pressure to always be right, always be perfect, always be just so.... When so much of

their energy becomes focused on how they look, it is very hard to focus on what they are thinking, what they ought to be doing for their futures, and even how they feel.

The challenge for us all is to ensure that women do not continue to be shunted aside into lower-paying jobs, made to feel as though they don't "belong" in any particular profession. To properly teach computer literacy, one must provide an educational climate that fosters inclusion. Those who believe that they do not belong are frozen out of the learning process, and those who are actively or passively discouraged from participation in the Information Age are unlikely to make the leap across the digital divide. "We are an increasingly technological society," said Ms. Orenstein, "so the fact that all over the country girls have less exposure to technology, are less comfortable with technology, are using technology less than boys is doing day-to-day, hour-by-hour damage to their future prospects."

This of course means a concerted effort on the part of educators as well as parents. Teachers need to be more aware of the ease with which these stereotypes can enter the classroom. "To create equality in the classroom a teacher really has to be paying attention to every single thing that's going on," said Vickie Dunlevy. "Once you're aware of what's happening, then you intervene by saying things such as 'the computer—today, everyone's going to have a turn at this.'" This type of approach will eventually benefit all involved. The active participation of girls in the classroom puts less stress on the boys to be the ones to always perform. Also, teachers benefit significantly from having a classroom in which everyone participates. "Teachers who begin to teach in an equitable way often report that they enjoy teaching so much more now because instead of having a few kids to interact with, they now have a lot of kids to interact with," explained Jo Sanders. "It's better for everyone, really."

DOUBLE STANDARDS DO NOT STOP with issues of classroom achievement. The gender stereotypes that exist in the classroom technological environment translate into a troubling lack of content in technology classes, on the internet, and a dearth of computer games that appeal directly to the interests or needs of girls. The gender gap must also be addressed outside of the academic environment. Fortunately, significant efforts are underway on many fronts to address the technological needs of girls and to help them to accept technology as a part of their lives. Individual efforts include the work of people like Heidi and Heather Swanson. These sisters have collaborated with several web producers to create the website ChickClick, an internet location that provides a self-described "pro-girl voice" that reaffirms girls' self-confidence, creating an empowering space for girls to explore and interact. "We want girls to be passionate about technology and we think we have a process in place that can help that," explains Heidi Swanson. "The idea that you can get on-line and communicate with all these different people on-line about all these different things is a lot more interesting to girls than sitting in front of a TV or a computer and battling a monster. They want to get on-line and communicate, and share their ideas, and feel supported and supportive."

Another positive sign is the increasing number of resources like Girl Tech, targeted at supporting girls' growth and interests in math, the sciences, and technology. "Girl Tech is all about encouraging girls in technology use," stated developer Janese Swanson, "and what we do is we build electronic toys or gadgets for girls, as well as a stellar website. . . . We want to validate girls and their contribution, and women and their contribution to our society, to make things different and better. We get girls from over eighty-five countries coming to our site, talking about what they do in their culture and what they do in their world, and we post that information. And it's wonderful to see the response. It's taken a few years to build it and now they're coming." These resources are also having a broader effect, enhancing an understanding of the issues girls face worldwide, and creating a setting where they can explore both the differences and similarities in their experiences, forming a basis for understanding the diversity of cultures and the similarity of the human experience.

Resources like ChickClick and Girl Tech allow girls to discover that they are not alone in their fears, feelings, and ideas in a nonthreatening environment, preparing them to take their new-found confidence to the world outside of the computer. "We show examples of girls that are creating exciting places on-line, put them all in one space, and hope that when a new girl comes to visit that she is going to want to participate," Heidi Swanson said. "That is when she will go in and say, 'How do I create my own site?'"

As this indicates, though, they need access to a computer, in a space where they can be relaxed enough to use it to communicate, in order to take advantage of this opportunity. And only about half of all U.S. households have computers. In order for young girls to successfully cross the digital divide, technology has to become an accepted part of their full life—school, work, and play. "If it's integrated in everything they do," noted software developer Janese Swanson, "then it doesn't cause fears and it just becomes second nature for girls to communicate and invest and share and learn and grow with that technology." Hence the need for more collective efforts to get girls involved.

TERRY HINER'S TECHGRRLZ AFTER-school course at Fulmore is a step toward this future. Hiner, a social studies teacher at Fulmore, began the technology program in 1997 as a way for girls throughout the school to find excitement and gain self-confidence with technology. Its appeal has been wide-ranging, from the generally computer-curious to jocks to those with discipline problems. The TechGrrlz setting allows girls to congregate as equals and to discuss topics that they would not feel comfortable discussing in the company of boys, such as computers. Sofia Shaikh, a Fulmore student from Pakistan, was already interested in computers at an early age. "When I came to America," she said, "I was really interested in computers because I didn't get to use them really frequently in Pakistan. So I was after my household to get me a computer." Eventually, Sofia's efforts were rewarded, but such interest combined with access to the technology at home makes a girl like Sofia the exception rather than the rule. Hence she saw TechGrrlz as an opportunity to meet other girls equally interested in computers. Now, she and fellow student Sarah Schulman get together regularly to search the internet and create interesting projects for their classwork. "She told me that she really loved computers and that is the same with me," she said of her friend Sarah. "And so we got together and worked on computers, and we went to TechGrrlz and we talked about things."

More common to the TechGrrlz group is a student like Melanie Loera, who enjoys being a part of the TechGrrlz community because it provides additional access to computer technology which she does not have at home. "I joined because I like to get on computers," she said. "The only time I get on computers is when [there is] that 'Take Your Daughter or Children to Work' week. And I only get to do that at my mom's work. And that was, like, once a year. And so, when I heard about this, I wanted to join because I thought that I could get on the computer more, learn a lot more."

Sometimes, though, it takes a little push to find out that there are options available to you. Gracie Reyes took the initiative to sign up her daughter, student Valerie Baeza, for the TechGrrlz program. "The first time I heard about TechGrrlz," said Ms. Reyes, "Valerie was getting in trouble . . . she was hanging around—I guess with the wrong crowd, and she was going bad, you know, she was missing work, she wasn't turning in her homework." While involved in the TechGrrlz program, Valerie started doing better in school. In an environment where she could just be who she was, and not be "on stage" for boys and peers, she was able to take advice she wasn't willing to accept before. "Miss Hiner kept saying in order to be what I wanted to be, I had to stay in school and I had to study," Valerie explained. Valerie believes having access to computers has made her a better student, and her mother has noticed the interest in technology that both

Valerie and her sister, Gabby, have acquired. "They love the computers, the internet, you know, they're always talking about they went into the internet. I mean, they love it," Ms. Reyes said. "Especially Gabby Baeza, she likes the computer way too much." This level of interest is typical of many young girls and indicates that programs like TechGrrlz can also help children realize their needs for the future.

The response to the TechGrrlz experience has been overwhelmingly positive. "There's an enormous sense of pride that they express," Ms. Hiner said of her students. "In the afternoons, I never know what they're going to want to do on the computers. They don't always want to follow a lesson plan that I've chosen for them, and, in fact, they're writing their own lessons. They're out there in this sort of brave new world of technology." Ms. Hiner, and many like her, believes that resources like TechGrrlz are necessary to give girls a space to work on being themselves, to explore their limits, and to have open interactions with other girls free from the influences inherent in mixed-gender groups. "There is no reason that a girl could not do anything that a guy can do using a mouse and a keyboard," she said. "There is no reason—nothing at all in the equipment itself, only what's in your head that might keep you from doing it. And what I'm hoping to do with TechGrrlz is break down those barriers in girls' heads."

Innovative resources like TechGrrlz, organized by creative and concerned teachers like Ms. Hiner, can be seen as models for larger-scale initiatives to help girls gain the confidence and the skills to succeed in the digital future. A good measure of their success is the appeal of such programs even outside their intended audience. At Fulmore, several older women visited

TechGrrlz one day, among them Ms. Hiner's mother, Betty Hiner. When asked why she came to TechGrrlz, she replied, "Well, because I am seventy years old and I do not want to become obsolete. So I am getting into computers."

Some experts believe that gender separation of this kind will not resolve the basic issues, no matter what happens in the segregated environment. "Let's say we make these girls really computer literate," suggests Jo Sanders, "and very sophisticated, and very knowledgeable, and very assertive. Then they get back in the world with a bunch of male people who still think that girls should be docile and quiet and ignorant. This is a solution?" While the best solution is obviously for men and women, boys and girls to change their perceptions of themselves and of each other, this represents a fundamental change in our cultural perspective that will take many years of dedicated effort to achieve. As it is, there are still some men and women who would rather not see it happen at all.

Although separate, all-girl environments may not be perfect, programs like Ms. Hiner's are models for constructive change. TechGrrlz and similar programs do not advocate a complete separation of the sexes. "I'm not advocating that girls go to girls-only schools," stated Ms. Hiner. "I'm not even advocating that all classes be gendered. But I think that occasionally, girls, particularly girls at this age, need a place that's girl-friendly, girl-safe, someplace they can just sort of be, and not be on for guys."

Students like Sarah Schulman agree wholeheartedly. "I think that's why TechGrrlz is so wonderful," she said, "because it's a setting where girls are supported, where they have friends and other girls to talk to, to share similar situations, to have a forum to express their ideas, along with learning the basics of technology."

Terry Hiner left Fulmore Middle School to take a position with SmartGrrls, an educational website for girls. Ms. Hiner's departure highlights the problem that public schools face in terms of losing technology-savvy teachers to competing organizations.

OTHER EFFORTS TO BRIDGE THE confidence gap are commercially based, drawing girls into becoming consumers of computer software or on-line services and products. In the software industry, a field that until very recently was almost exclusively run by, with, and for males, female voices have been few and far between. Nancie S. Martin, now a Director at Mattel Media-Software for Girls, a game software division of Mattel Toy Co., heads a division that was almost unimaginable ten years ago. "When I started in the multimedia business in 1991," she said, "what I found was that I would go to meetings, I would go to conferences, and I would often be the only woman in the room." A lone voice, Ms. Martin ran into the expected biases and distortions of the potential for a girls' market. "People had said girls don't like computers, they're afraid of technology, they're not really interested. Some people said, 'Well, we already tried that and it didn't work.' And really what they had tried was doing a shoot 'em up video game and making all the characters pink."

A piece of software aimed directly at the "girl" market, "Barbie Fashion Designer," proved once and for all that girls would buy computer software. In its first two months on the market, "Fashion Designer" sold more than 500,000 copies, a respectable return on investment for any game software targeted at any audience. "Once they made that hit, it cracked open a lot of doors," explained software developer Ernest Adams. "And it cracked open a lot of minds in the industry, because the success of Barbie told people who otherwise would not have given girls the time of day that there is money to be made here."

This success, however, also has its share of controversy. Critics claim that an unintended consequence of software for girls could be the creation of a restrictive niche market, essentially using software marketing to enforce preconceived stereotypes. Take, for instance, an issue as seemingly superficial as that of package labeling. In a presumptive effort to target girl consumers and increase girls' participation, some people have suggested putting a "software for girls" label on the boxes of products designed to appeal specifically to girls. While putting this label onto packaging may indeed draw girls to the box, it may also, by extension, channel them away from more substantial and more challenging software that also enhance their capabilities and self-image. "I think little kids, in particular, have very distinct notions about sex roles that are no longer appropriate, but they form them automatically themselves and they decide that if something is right for one sex role, it is not right for the other," said Ernest Adams. "And so by saying 'software for girls,' that will encourage little kids to think that the rest of the software is not for girls. . . . It makes them believe that this is all they are allowed to have. . . . I think it has not yet been tested whether that [gender-specific play] is the only way to get girls interested in computing. I think there are other ways of getting girls interested in computing that are about larger dreams, larger aspirations, larger fantasies."

Software targeted for girls should, ideally, encourage them to explore not just technology but also their own identities. "We need to build more products and services that encourage girls in these different areas and show them that again, it's about celebrating our differences. And we're very different among our gender," said software developer Janese Swanson. "Having all these different options for play and trying on roles and seeing if it fits and if it doesn't, move on to the next thing— that's really critical and important." Progress continues to be made on how best to engage girls to enhance their abilities and experience with computers and in finding their voice in cyberspace. Purple Moon, a software company that aims its products primarily at adolescent girls, has done significant research, starting in 1992, on the differences between the play patterns of boys and girls, and what sort of preferences girls might have in computer play. "The key finding was that the main reason they don't like traditional computer games is not that they're too violent or too competitive, but that they're too boring," said Brenda Laurel, the vice president at Purple Moon in charge of design. "And when you ask what you mean by that, the answer is the characters aren't interesting, there is no story, this isn't relevant to me, there's no personal relevance."

The culmination of this research identifies two main areas of interest for girls, social play and private fantasy play. As a result, Purple Moon has created a series of software titles involving social play ("Rockett's New School," "Rockett's Tricky Decision," and "Rockett's Adventure Maker," among others) that allows girls to participate in a realistic environment, and invites them to try out different responses to social situations and get feedback. They have also created a title for fantasy play, "Secret Path in the Forest." Finally, Purple Moon has climbed aboard the girls' sports bandwagon with "The Starfire Soccer Challenge."

Purple Moon was purchased in 1999 by Mattel, showing the problems faced by smaller independent companies. What Mattel will ultimately do with the company is the subject of much speculation, but the newest Rockett software has a different look and feel than the previous ones developed by Purple Moon.

Many designers are rethinking games for girls to reflect this new information. The variety of concepts run the gamut from growth and physical changes, to friends and family, to romance. Girl Games, Inc., in Austin, Texas, is a software company that has created products entitled "Let's Talk About Me" and "Let's Talk About Me! Some More" which focus on a girl's life, personality, body, and future. There has also been a successful companion book to the two software titles. "'Let's Talk About Me' is the quintessential game for a girl," said Laura Groppe, the President of Girl Games. "It is the handbook to surviving the torture of adolescence. And it was the very first product to really blow out a new play paradigm, a new kind of interface, a new way of using the computer to play. And the content is basically every thing to do with a girl."

The internet and related computer technology represents an entirely new forum for girls and women to access information, interact with others, create content, and gain the confidence and competence to go on to further success in their lives. In many ways, the Information Age represents a back-to-square-one situation for both men and women, a chance for girls to learn the tools needed in the digital workplace and be on an equal technological footing with boys, and for boys and girls to learn to work together cooperatively, with mutual respect, as they will have to in this new workplace. But all of us together, as parents, teachers, and members of society's institutions, must support girls' entry into this arena. If we want the future to be bright for our daughters in the Information Age, then we must create an environment where girls are welcome to explore, to fantasize about different careers for themselves, and to gain the confidence and expertise to make those dreams come true. "I think that the more comfortable girls are using it [the computer]," said Carol Burger, the former director of the program for women and girls at the National Science Foundation, "and the better materials that are on the computer for them to access, the more likely it is that they'll feel comfortable in thinking of themselves as a technical person, as someone who could be a computer science major, as someone who could be a programmer."

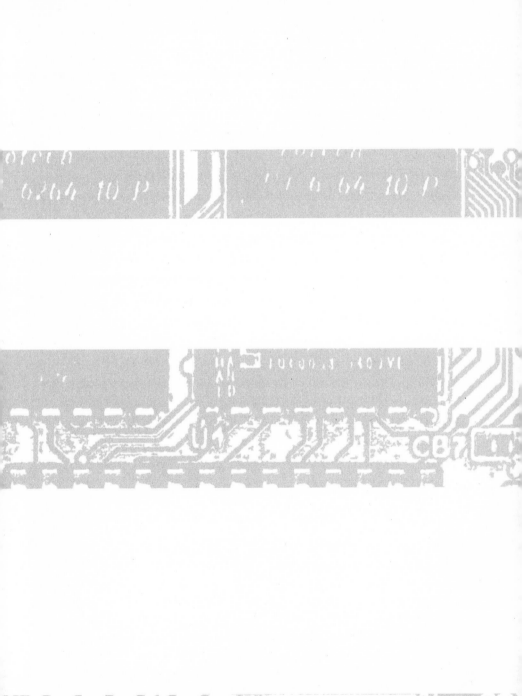

4

The World
White Web

In July 1999, the Department of Commerce released *Falling Through the Net: Defining the Digital Divide*, the third annual federal survey statistically showing who is using the digital tools of today. The study found that 26.2 percent of U.S. homes now have internet access, an increase of over 40 percent from two years earlier. Access to computers has increased across the board: up 52.8 percent among European-American homes, 52 percent for African-American ones, and 48.3 percent for Latinos. Yet despite the fact that we are reaching a point where more than fifty percent of American homes will have computers, the digital divide is, in fact, widening. Computer ownership among European-American households is 46.6 percent, while the rate for minority groups like Latinos is only 25.5 percent. African-American and Latino households are less than half as likely as European-American families to have internet access anywhere—on the job, at home, or in school.

The Department of Commerce's findings are confirmed by many other studies, and statistics like these speak volumes about the state of computer technology distribution in America. The Benton Foundation's study *Losing Ground Bit by Bit* also indicates that, while over 80 percent of families with incomes of $100,000 or more have computers at home, only about 25 percent of those households with annual incomes under $30,000 have home access to computers. Demographically, this means that the digital revolution is in full swing in America's wealthy suburbs and affluent sections of cities and towns, while in some of our poorest areas, it is a phenomenon that is at best heard about on television.

Yet income alone is not the primary factor in determining computer ownership. At the lowest income levels, the gap has widened considerably for computer ownership among racial minorities when compared with European-Americans. In the context of the overall racial digital divide, a low-income European-American child is three times more likely to have internet access than his or her African-American counterpart, and four times as likely as a Latino family in the same socio-economic category. While African-Americans and Latinos represent about 1 in 5 American households, they represent only about 1 in 10 "netizens," or households that are on-line and using the internet.

Granted, these reports show that all racial groups are getting on the internet in greater numbers. When you look more closely, though, the issue is not one of quantity but of distribution. While it is true that more African-Americans are getting on-line, a disturbing gap remains in contrast to European-Americans: between 1994 and 1998, this gap grew from 16.8 to 23.4 percent. A study conducted by professor Donna Hoffman at Vanderbilt University—who is also co-director of Project 2000, a corporate-sponsored research center devoted to the study of commercializing emerging media (like the World Wide

Web)—places the increase rate of African-American involvement at only 12 percent versus a 38 percent increase for European-Americans in the mid-1990s. Additionally, internet use is much less common in minority communities. In a recent six-month period, 36 percent of European-Americans had been on the internet. In that same period, only 28 percent of Hispanic-Americans and 22 percent of African-Americans had accessed on-line services. During the eighteen-month period ending in June 1998, the figures for the number of people on-line had increased by 60 percent for European-American users, but only 11 percent for Hispanic-Americans and 32 percent for African-Americans. Figures like these show that, while computer use in general is on the rise, the digital divide between European-Americans and other racial groups is actually increasing, despite numerous efforts to create awareness and provide equipment and training.

There has been much speculation among internet analysts as to the reasons for the lower rates of participation on-line among communities of color. Some note past restrictions on education, employment, housing, and other basic needs in minority communities that have created sets of negative expectations. These have carried over to the field of technology, as the internet has been up to now almost entirely the province of European-American males. "One of the things we found that was very surprising," noted Ms. Hoffman, "was that when whites and African-Americans do not have a computer in the home, whites are still more likely to use the computer. In fact this difference was dramatic, and [whites were] much more likely to use the internet than were African-Americans." Hoffman's study indicates that, for income levels below

$40,000, 39 percent of European-American households had internet access, while only 19 percent of African-American households at this income level had access.

Ms. Hoffman sees attention being given to media other than computers in minority communities. "Personal computer prices have dropped dramatically," she said, "and African-Americans' adoption of satellite technology and cable is dramatic. We think there are social and cultural factors that are influencing certain segments of society so they don't feel that they are interested in adopting PCs." It's not that minority groups, as some people have claimed, aren't as interested in technology. Ms. Hoffman's study indicates quite the opposite. "One of the things that we found was that African-Americans were much more likely to want access to the internet than were whites," she explained.

Rather, the issue seems related to a lack of identification with the digital future among most minority members. For the most part, when minority youths go to a software store or log onto the internet, they do not see reflections of themselves. "People intellectually know that [technology] is something they need," stated Trish Millines Dziko, founder of the Technology Access Foundation, which works with children from diverse communities. "But then on the other side, it is still something that white people do. When you talk to kids, it is something that the white kids do, because that is all they see." Moreover, as Ms. Millines Dziko states, the situation is the same when they look outside of the classroom:

> You know, you say, "Who is a scientist? What does a scientist look like? What does a computer repair per-

son look like?" You know, they'll almost always draw a white person and it's always a man. It's the same stuff they see in advertisements. It's the same things they see on TV. In their community, maybe. They need to have a little variety in role models who are willing to spend time with them, not just stand in front of them and say, "Well, I build computers." And then that is the end of that.

This phenomenon is reflected in a significant lack of content on-line that is of interest to African-Americans. Ms. Hoffman and others have attributed this lack of content to the low numbers of computer owners in the minority communities. The power of the internet is not only the accessibility of content, but the communication of knowledge. This knowledge transfer can be more than simply data, it can also be the cultural awareness it provides. "Even though there are important differences between whites and African-Americans with respect to their access and their usage," stated Ms. Hoffman, "there are still a significant proportion of African-Americans on-line, suggesting that it's very important to continue efforts to develop content, targeted not only toward that group, but in general recognizing that they're a very important media opportunity." Culturally then, the internet enables awareness as the public display of cultural differences appear on the World Wide Web. And this cultural experience can translate itself into market opportunities, giving minority groups that have previously been underrepresented in the business community the ability to pull themselves up by their own bootstraps, *if* they can make an appeal to their consumer segment, and if that appeal is heard.

The content theory, while part of the problem, may only go so far in showing the full picture. B. Keith Fulton, the director for technology programs and policy at the National Urban League, agrees that there is "a tendency for the typical kind of content you might find on the internet [being] content that reflects the early adopters. They were primarily scientists, professors, largely white males, and so the content tended to be of an academic or scientific nature." However, he believes that a climate of fear and alienation surrounding technology in the African-American community may also be to blame:

> There are two schools of thought. One is that, for African-Americans, our historical experience with automation has been one of disengagement and disenfranchisement. From the automation of plantations to industrialization in the North, whenever automation has come it's been to the disadvantage of African-Americans, so there is a lot of distrust there. Phones, cable TV, these are proven technologies. The second school of thought says that, for African-American kids, teachers aren't as well trained, schools don't have as many computers; kids aren't bringing the demand home for parents to get this device.

Omar Wasow, a noted internet analyst, agrees that content alone is not the source of the problem. "I think that is, maybe, too narrow a definition of who black people are," he said. "Black people invest in stocks, are interested in today's news, are curious about all manner of things that aren't specifically about being black. I think, in fact, black people, like everybody else, are photographers and cat lovers and Christians, and seek out those areas of interest to them.... [And] you'll see more and more people filling the voids where they see them. So that if I am a black Christian cat lover, then I'll create that forum because that's what I want."

Mr. Wasow hopes the creation of newer sites like BET.com and NetNoir will increase the rate of on-line activity among the African-American community. Black Entertainment Television (BET) Holdings Inc. recently spent $35 million to launch BET.com, a portal that will offer a full array of services, from electronic mail to shopping and other services targeted at African-Americans. The BET website has assembled a broad array of big players in the technology field for financial support, from Microsoft to Rupert Murdoch's News America Digital Publishing. BET Chairman Robert L. Johnson sees the website as filling a direct need in the African American community. "We have come together to ensure that African-American consumers are not left out of the economy," he said. The site will rely on the high profile of other BET divisions in television, cable, and print to ensure its success. However, unlike BET's broadcast and cablecast operations, which do not currently face rival African-American channels, the website already faces several rivals. NetNoir and BlackVoices.com preceded BET.com, the former by several years. David Ellington, the founder of NetNoir, is encouraged by the growing popularity of websites like his. "Black folks will embrace the technology of the internet as soon as it becomes more relevant to our lives," he explained.

New web portals are also being created to serve Latino communities, who as a group fall even further behind European-Americans than African-Americans in computer literacy. A recent survey by the Public Policy Institute of California (*San Francisco Chronicle*, September 13, 1999, pp. A17–18) found that, despite an increase in technology access, computer use among California's Hispanic-Americans still lagged behind their European-American counterparts—this, despite the fact that Hispanics represent one quarter of the population. There was an even larger gap in internet usage, with only 39 percent of Hispanic-Americans indicating any use of the internet, versus 65 percent for European-Americans. Home ownership of computers showed similar differences.

The lower numbers in the Latino communities can be attributed in part to the fact that English is still the primary language of the internet. This, coupled with a dearth of Spanish-language information about, and advertising for, computers (a conclusion supported by findings of the Tomas Rivera Policy Center in the report *Buying into the Computer Age: A Look at Hispanic Families*) represents a significant hurdle even for those willing and able to join the digital revolution. But some new sites are attempting to address the language barrier, providing much the same content as one could find on mainstream portals such as Yahoo! but with multilingual options. New sites such as LatinoLink and Picosito are now providing service to specific communities that have suffered from a lack of access and identity on the internet in the past. StarMedia Network recently launched a web portal aimed at Spanish-speaking internet users. This new portal, Periscopio, differs from an older StarMedia site that focused on the typical community-type content for portals (chat, e-mail, and message boards). As an alternative to such standard fare, Periscopio is centered on web searching and current events. Periscopio, LatinoLink, and Picosito are, in turn, facing competition from a new Spanish-language website created by Yahoo! and another under construction at AOL.

Although these new sites are a continued reflection of the growing sense of technological empowerment among minorities, computer literacy needs to flourish at a more advanced rate if we ever hope to close the digital divide. In order to ensure that African-American and Latino children are not left out of the digital future, we will have to look to many sectors of our society, from schools to businesses to community organizations, for help. "In fifteen years, if we're looking around and African-Americans or Latinos or anyone else is saying, 'Hey, how did we get left out?,'" warns Tariq Muhammad, the Technology Editor of *Black Enterprise* magazine, "it will be because today we didn't do enough to ensure that we and our children and our children's children were masters and creators of this information technology revolution, as opposed to mere consumers."

KRYSTAL PEREZ IS A PUERTO RICAN student in the New York public school system. Like many young Latinos, Krystal does not have a computer at home. She uses the computer in her school library—when she can get access to it. "When I can't get time on the computer it makes me feel bad," said Krystal, "because you know, I did a good job writing the first draft and a couple of drafts of the exhibitions and the reports, and I feel so bad that I can't have it in my portfolio typed up." Although Krystal may not receive a lower grade because her report is not typed, she is still at a disadvantage. "To do my homework and my exhibitions and reports," she said, "I have to go to the library." As her assignments become more important and more complex, her disadvantage will become that much more pronounced.

Krystal's situation is often the norm for the technologically disenfranchised. The Department of Commerce's study found that those who are less likely to have computer and internet access at home or work are relying more frequently on public resources such as schools, libraries, and community technology centers. Over 35 percent of Latinos who access the internet outside the home are likely to go on-line at public schools; for rural Latinos, this figure rises to over 46 percent.

The problems of relying solely on public institutions for computer and internet access is that proper time and resources are scarce, especially in minority communities. This discrepancy in *community* access gets at the heart of the racial digital divide. "When we poked a little further into these results," said Donna Hoffman of her Project 2000 study, "we found that . . . whites, but not African-Americans, are much more likely to have access at non-traditional locations . . . for example community centers, libraries with internet access, using computers at friends' and relatives' houses, and so on. And we felt that this was an extremely disquieting result because it's suggesting very clearly that we do not have equity in our communities with respect to this very important technological innovation."

This fact is well known to Kevin Allard-Mendelson, Director of Technology for the Brooklyn Public Library. The library has made an extensive effort to provide computers to the community, but Mr. Allard-Mendelson recognizes the limitations inherent in this approach. "Are the efforts that schools and libraries make to deliver technology to students enough?" he asked. "No, I think that they're not. At the current time, specifically in large urban environments, you have an average of a forty-five minute instructional period during which students have access to a computer lab. And in a library, we have half-hour time slots. And perhaps you can get one every day, or one every other day. That's still not enough time to really become acclimated to the technology, understand it, and be able to use it effectively." Using a library computer or one at an after-school program is simply not the same as having the access, as well as the convenience and privacy, that home use provides.

This is not to suggest that public organizations don't have a role to play. Twenty years ago, the difference between the opportunities for children in rich communities and poor communities might have been measured by the disparities in their athletic facilities or libraries. Today, it is measured in terms of the quantity and quality of their computer technology and their staff's training at public institutions. The difference is that poor athletic facilities may only affect one aspect of a young person's life experience. But if a community lags behind in terms of computers, the lack is felt in every aspect of the lives of the young people there. Many communities are trying to do something about this state of affairs through the creation of public facilities of one kind or another. "For many individuals in our society, particularly students, and for poor students, and poor minority students who are in worse shape with respect to access and use in this country," explained Donna Hoffman, "it'll be very important to stimulate local access points. For example, through community centers, through libraries with internet access, and things of that nature."

With public libraries limited in their ability to provide the necessary resources, non-profit organizations are stepping in to help. "Universal access is great, in theory," said Anthony Lopez, Executive Director of the civil rights organization ASPIRA in New York City. "However, when resources for universal access are targeted to schools and public libraries, our young people do not have access to these institutions if they go to sign up for use of a work station and the wait list is so long. It really translates to no access. Therefore, we think it's important, if universal access is truly going to be universal, it must include a role for non-profit organizations, as well as Latino community-based organizations." Organizations like ASPIRA and the Urban League nationwide regard the digital divide as a civil rights issue and are teaming up with organizations like community technology centers to make a political statement about the role that digital technology can play in advancing a more diverse culture in America.

As a result, community technology centers, or CTCs, are becoming neighborhood focal points that provide computer access and training for young people and adults. As part of what B. Keith Fulton calls "the modern community infrastructure," CTCs help provide the means by which people in the inner cities are helping themselves out of the social safety net. As people move beyond their experiences and expectations regarding poverty, discrimination, and hopelessness, they need places to go and something to do when they get there. CTCs are safe harbors from which to start that journey.

The East Harlem Tutorial Program is one of these CTCs. Like other CTCs throughout the country, it provides computer access and training for young people and adults, along with job- and life-skills training. Carmen Vega-Rivera is executive director of the tutorial program there, which is attended by both Krystal Perez and her mother Iris. "Our children won't have marketable skills if they don't have access to the computers," said Ms. Vega-Rivera, explaining the role played by CTCs like hers. "And you will find them taking on the jobs that no one else wants to take on, which is working in a fast-food restaurant and cleaning up after someone else."

Another CTC, The Urban Technology Center has, as executive director Patricia S. Bransford described it, a mission "to provide access to technology to those people in inner-city communities who had formerly been overlooked or underserved." Ms. Bransford began the center three years ago. "At that point we were 14 percent in terms of use and the white population was close to 30," she stated. "We were very troubled by that gap and we felt that if that continued that it would further cause economic problems, social problems, in the United States, and so we put the Urban Technology Center together." The Center provides a supportive learning environment as much through a methodology of empowerment as through a methodology of skills transfer.

CTCs address a central problem that has long troubled B. Keith Fulton. "There's a subtle difference in the digital divide that people may not appreciate," observes Mr. Fulton, "but in some schools in more affluent communities the children are more likely to work in groups, use a computer as a discovery tool, and they're doing exploration, and they're figuring out a problem. They're developing the kind of mental skills that help them to go out and be leaders in our society." The Urban League has the oldest and largest CTCs in the country. The Los Angeles Urban League built the nation's first CTC in 1968, in the aftermath of the Watts riots. The Urban League recently announced the creation of five new CTCs in Aurora, Illinois; Cleveland; Detroit; Indianapolis; and Milwaukee. One of the oldest civil rights organizations in the country, the National Association for the Advancement of Colored People (NAACP), recently announced a partnership with AT&T that will provide technology centers in twenty cities nationwide. "The technological segregation known as the digital divide must be narrowed," NAACP President Kweisi Mfume said upon the occasion of the announcement of this initiative.

In the inner cities, though, accessibility does equate to a capability or the time to learn. Inner-city families who are trying to support households are more likely than not to contain a single parent with several children and an income from one or even two jobs. In situations like this, non-profit organizations like Concord Family Services serve a crucial role. Concord Family Services is a foster-care agency that partnered with Urban Technologies in Brooklyn to create a community technology center. The purpose of the partnership is to raise awareness of the necessity for training the next generation of workers in computer-related skills, and providing that training. Shaquana Davis, a foster child in the program, is learning computer skills at Concord's CTC, as her school, in one of America's largest and most prosperous cities, does not have the computer resources. "No, I don't have computers at my school," she said, "but I wish I had computers at my school because the kids at my school ask me about computers, and I tell them about the computers and what you can do on there. And they ask me can I get things off the computer [at Concord Family Services] and I get it off the computer for them."

Many children like Shaquana benefit from the programs at Concord Family Services. Working one-on-one with an Urban Tech staff member, she begins developing hands-on technology skills, an important first step toward job opportunities in the computer industry. "I learned how to repair computers through the leadership academy program," she said. "I installed a hard drive, a CD-ROM. And I installed a sound card and a modem. And I installed Windows 95 on the computer today." This represents not only a shift of skill sets beyond her forebears, but a sense of self-assurance and pride of accomplishment.

Shaquana has found that some of her friends are envious of the knowledge that has been made readily available to her. Her experiences have a ripple effect on those around her. She learns from the people at Family Services. She tells and hopefully teaches the kids at school about those experiences and about computers and connecting to the on-line world. Maybe she puts up a web page and communicates with other people beyond her immediate geographical area. The more she does this, the deeper the impact. The deeper the impact, the stronger the ripples, and the longer the duration. So access increases interest and more interest becomes more involvement. It's natural, and it's human nature, and this technology can allow people to interact in ever-widening circles.

Community-based solutions like these are a wonderful first step in overcoming the digital divide and ideally will contribute to more home ownership and use in minority communities. But maintaining community commitments to technology centers can be difficult. Ultimately, it's the same dilemma facing our schools. Merely acquiring technology is only the first step. Equally important is a strategy for effective use of that technology that incorporates long-term maintenance, upgrades, and technical support. "In building the kind of centers that we build, it takes a significant investment and resources," explained B. Keith Fulton. "There's machines, connectivity, there's people resources, and one of the biggest challenges once you get the money is keeping it going. Now, you give me a big grant and I can build a center. One of the biggest challenges is making sure that center is there two years from now, three years from now, five years from now."

THE RACIAL DIGITAL DIVIDE EXISTS at every income level save the very highest. Yet, some writers persist in hoping that this divide will disappear over time. There are some analysts who decry the entire notion of a "racial digital divide." A common theme among these critics is that the digital divide is tied strictly to income levels, and that the divide will disappear due to market forces making computers more accessible through decreased costs. Some writers characterize the declining cost of computers by stating that "pricing is following the natural progression of luxury items in a free society." Others observe that "not everyone has a washing machine." This perspective depicts computers as mere consumer conveniences, not unlike a microwave oven.

But the evidence is overwhelming that computers are essential educational and vocational tools, not luxurious frivolities. As a society, we have taken steps to ensure that all citizens have access to those things that are critical to modern life. We have "lifeline" rates for phone service so that the elderly and poor can use phones to communicate in emergencies and we have government-provided freeways, not private toll roads. Surely ensuring access to computers for our citizens is more akin to lifeline rates and freeways, than to frivolous luxury items.

Resolving the issues brought up by the digital divide requires a two-sided agreement: from the educational establishment, the government, and corporate America, assuming responsibility for providing proper resources; from individuals, taking responsibility for motivating and applying themselves to get an education. "The real factor here is education," stressed Omar Wasow. "That's where the divide occurs. And how it plays itself out with computers is simply a manifestation or a magnification of that. People who are well-educated do very well in an information economy. People who are poorly educated struggle." Education needs to provide a grounding in literacy and its corollary, information literacy, which expands on literacy and encompasses a variety of interrelated skills.

B. Keith Fulton believes that in a way the results of computer and internet access are more important than the means of access. "What's really critical about having access is not just the access in and of itself, it's what you do with it," he said. " Can kids read better? Can they do better in school? Are adults getting living-wage jobs? Those kinds of things are the results that we're hoping for as people access these new technologies...owning a computer, accessing the web at a community center, are the kinds of things that will lend themselves to building information literacy. There's a new basic, and it's called information literacy."

According to Mr. Fulton, the future success of our children is dependent on this new form of literacy, which is not acquired in place of other, more traditional, forms of literacy. On the contrary, one kind is inherently connected to the other. Access is only one of the tools in building this information literacy, which extends beyond reading to include such skills as comprehension and critical thinking. "In the information age, it is critically important to master the three basics: reading, writing, and arithmetic," stated Mr. Fulton, "but also to have information literacy: the ability to access, interpret, and respond to information. Information literacy assumes access." One of the reasons that this disparity in skill levels is growing is because teachers in rural areas, in the inner cities, and on the Native American reservations are not equipped to encompass that broader spectrum of ideas and practices. They are teaching individual subjects, not integrated curriculums. "I think if that kind of disparity remains," warned Mr. Fulton, "then we risk a further-widening gap between the haves and the have-nots at a time where our society is going through an epochal shift in its position in the world economy."

"It's a very troubling notion," confirmed Omar Wasow, "because what you're seeing is that people are putting computer literacy before literacy, and they're confusing the importance of being able to read, write, and think critically with the ability to manipulate a machine." When you put computer literacy before literacy, the only thing you are doing is turning out people who do not have a complete facility with either. The computer, for all of its audio and graphic capabilities, is still primarily a written medium, words on a screen. If people cannot create readable, understandable, and relevant content, then having a computer is of little or no value to them. As Wasow put it, "Computers are only as useful as . . . your ability to make good decisions and to sort of use this tool as an extension of your mind."

Information literacy is like a three-legged table. Without each of those three legs—literacy, computer skills, and access—the table just falls over. The Information Age is not just about computer literacy. If schools are not producing literate students who can read, write, and generally express their ideas capably, let alone students with computer skills and experience gathering and analyzing information from the internet, those students will graduate to an unreceptive marketplace. "The implications are profound," stated Donna Hoffman, "because without access for all Americans we are going to see increasing problems. . . . We are not going to have a well-trained cadre of high-tech workers in this country and we will continue to see income gaps."

"Increasingly in the twenty-first century, the literacy line will be the essential barrier," foresees Mr. Wasow. "What we will need to ask is not 'how is race and racism holding people back?' It's 'how is illiteracy holding people back?'" A lack of literacy affects everything a person might hope to do, from being able to read instructions to being able to write on the computer to being able to communicate with other people. Work is moving in the direction of cooperative groups operating together to achieve company goals. If you cannot communicate with the group, you cannot work with the group.

Our schools are the logical places to usher in the Information Age. How we address the current set of problems in our school—illiteracy, low performance, dropout rates—are as important as what we put in place to create computer-knowledgeable workers who will fill positions in the digital workplace. "I think children of color in low-income communities do not get a good general education," said Ms. Dziko. "I think that we are just talking about basics here. . . . I think there are some survival instincts that would go well in corporate America, but first you have to have the skills to get there, and I think that is where the disconnect is. . . . The schools aren't preparing the kids, there is not enough money."

THE NATIONAL DIALOGUE ON EDUCATION must also emphasize that education, encompassing all information literacy skills, does not end when we graduate from high school or college. Industry in the digital revolution demands that adults continually learn and update their skills and outlook simply in order to maintain, let alone advance, their social and economic status. "The ramifications are enormous in terms of jobs and where minorities will be in the new millennium," said B. Keith Fulton. Many observers would agree that continual neglect of these issues will result in considerably diminished career paths for those who end up on the deprived side of the digital divide.

Countless well-meaning educators have directed minority children towards a career in technology. Bill Gates, for instance, recently provided one billion dollars for minority scholarships for careers in science and technology. Despite such generosity, though, the field of technology has a bad track record when it comes to hiring and promoting people of color.

Silicon Valley, the center of the technology world, has a hiring record that is particularly embarrassing. The *San Francisco Chronicle* published the results of a study in 1998 that put African-Americans at 4 percent of the workforce of the Valley and Latinos at 7 percent. Jesse Jackson inaugurated the Silicon Valley Project recently to, in his words, "seek full inclusion and diversity in the high-tech industry."

Silicon Valley is not alone in having a bleak track record when it comes to hiring people of color. Organizations such as the Black Data Processing Association and the Professional, Technical, and Diversity Network also work for greater diversity in the workforce of technology companies around the country. Only 5.4 percent of all computer programmers and 7.1 percent of computer systems analysts are African-American. Latinos hold 4.6 and 2.5 percent of these jobs, respectively.

Many technology company boosters take issue with the characterization of high-tech companies as being too homogenous. Harris Miller, the president of The Information Technology Association of America, a trade organization of eleven thousand technology companies, views the digital divide as "The Digital Opportunity." He touts market forces as the tool for eventually closing the gap between the haves and have-nots through decreasing computer costs. Mr. Miller cites a lack of educated applicants as the reason why more minorities are not hired by member companies. He and others point to the Computer Research Association's 1998 Taulbee Survey as proof that his industry is not engaging in discriminatory behavior. The survey could identify only sixteen doctorates in computer science awarded to African-Americans or Latinos and less than 3 percent of undergraduate computer science degrees awarded were given to African-Americans or Latinos. Of course, they fail to mention that the total number granted in 1998 was 933, or about one Ph.D. for every twelve member companies of the ITAA. Obviously, they are hiring a lot of people who do not have doctorates. And this also ignores the fact that the ITAA has done almost nothing to alleviate the current labor shortages by appealing to underrepresented groups, instead filling open positions with foreign workers.

In 1999, the original hiring quota for high-tech corporations of 65,000 foreign workers was raised to 115,000. There is talk now of raising it again to 200,000 (ZDNet News, June 7, 1999, by Maria Seminerio), a figure roughly equivalent to adding a city the size of Spokane, Washington, to the U.S. every year. Although there continues to be much talk about establishing training programs for citizens, in the year since the last round of visa increases the government has done nothing. Where does that leave the many U.S. citizens who would willingly fill these positions if they had access to the equipment and training to enter this job market?

Former Assistant Secretary of the U.S. Department of Commerce Larry Irving sees the hiring situation as a widespread problem. "I see people, in my job, every day who want to go invest billions of dollars in countries where the per capita income is one-tenth the per capita income at the low end of America's black and brown communities," he said. "It's racism. It's a lack of understanding of the commercial opportunities and it's a fear of the unknown."

If everyone is expected to learn computer skills and use them, there is an expectation that there will be jobs for them to go to. Corporations need to broaden their perspectives on who is hirable and how these prospective employees are going to develop the required skills. Trish Millines Dziko suggests that corporations get involved with schools as early as the primary years. "I think what makes sense is for them [corporations] to go K-12," she said. "Obviously you can't look at a kindergartner and decide that they can work for your company, but kids can legally work at the age of fourteen. So if you start them early enough, by the time they are fourteen you can teach them more advanced things. They can come and work at your corporation." As we have seen, this kind of School-to-Work model may, ideally, have very beneficial effects in low-income communities. "While before a certain age," she continued, "it is not appropriate to look at future work skills, it is appropriate to look at what type of skills, such as literacy and creative and critical thinking, kids need to learn so that when they get into the upper grades, it facilitates their learning to use both computers and software."

AS SOURCES OF INFORMATION move ever increasingly to the World Wide Web, those without access will not have access to new educational, communication, or entertainment possibilities. "In the information age, in the new age, if you don't have a computer, it is not 'have' and 'have not.' It is 'can' and 'can not,'" claims Marc R. Benioff, a senior vice president at Oracle Corp. "Because if you don't have access to information technology, you can not. You can not educate yourself. You can not communicate. You can not entertain yourself. You can not conduct commerce." With the increasing interconnectedness of entertainment, news, research, and information generally, more and more people may be forced out of the loop. You are either going to be there or not.

As a result, access and fluency on computers not only makes for a more informed student, but a more informed citizen. "Information is power," stated Trish Millines Dziko. "And equal access to computers will get you that information. And I think no longer will people be in the dark. People will learn about investing. They will learn about what's going on in their neighborhoods. They become more interested and so then they seek more information. So they vote more and they run for office more."

Ideas, innovation, and advances that help all of society know no specific language or skin color. What a true embodiment of diversity means is that all segments of our society have the ability to share points of view, to discuss differences, to agree to be in accord or to disagree, to develop a tolerance for ideas and influences different from our own, and to celebrate both our differences and our similarities. The true digital revolution rests in this movement towards each other and to acceptance and inclusiveness. Computers, software, and the internet are simply tools. How we use these tools, who gets to use them, and what the overall consequences of that use will be are decisions within our grasp. We have only to choose to speak up and make our voices heard.

Conclusion

S peaking with the voices of many people from across the country, *Digital Divide* looks at the role which computers are playing in widening socioeconomic and educational gaps throughout our society. The stark reality is that the majority of American youths are not conversant with digital tools, and their options may be increasingly bleak as a result.

We all know that the clock cannot be turned back, that digital technology is likely to increasingly shape the kind of country we live in. Rather than looking at technology as either good or bad, this book and the PBS series examine how technology intersects with race, gender, and class. These distinctions have haunted our republic from its origins. Now, access to and use of computers threaten to widen these differences in dramatic new ways.

There are many aspects of the digital divide that educators and community activists will find make for powerful instigators of discussion. One current reality is that the salary gap between the highest- and lowest-skilled workers in our society is increasing. Data from the U.S. Census and Department of Labor have shown that, for the period from 1969 to 1989, constant-dollar earnings for low-skilled male workers dropped by 24 percent, while the earnings for those at the top increased by 13 percent. It has not been the case that a rising economic tide raises all boats. In fact, jobs at the bottom of the pay ladder are disappearing at a prodigious rate; they are being automated or shipped to other countries where salaries are even lower.

Another reality is an information/communication gap. While it is the case that roughly 45 percent of U.S. homes have computers, studies by the Census Bureau have shown that computer access is strongly correlated to household income. As a rule of thumb, current computer penetration into homes can be estimated by taking family income in thousands of dollars per year and expressing the number as the percent of homes with computers. In other words, 70 percent of homes with a combined income of $70,000 or higher have computers, and 10 percent of homes with a combined income of $10,000 have computers in them. The numbers follow a nearly linear progression for intermediate income levels and hold pretty well independent of whether the communities are rural, urban, or suburban.

The digital divide is real, and the financial have-nots are also the informational have-nots. Given the importance of information technologies in the future, this gap can produce a permanent underclass and further expand the gap between the haves and the have-nots. For this reason alone it is essential that access to powerful information technologies is provided in every classroom, library, and other places where people from all backgrounds gather.

Unlike the internet, which is doubling in size every year, the World Wide Web—the portion of the internet generally used by the public—is doubling in size every ninety days. And even the use of the Web pales in comparison with electronic mail. In 1996, the U.S. Postal Service delivered 185 billion pieces of first-class mail. In that same year the internet handled about 1 trillion e-mail messages. Given that much of this internet traffic originated from homes, schools, and small businesses using ordinary voice-grade telephone lines, one can only imagine what will happen when broadband services become commonplace.

The impact of the web on education and in every aspect of our communities is likely to be profound. The internet is already being used to give students access to the latest breakthroughs in scientific discovery years before they are likely to appear in textbooks. Furthermore, students can perform their own research on various topics and post their results on the Web for other students, teachers, and researchers to see and evaluate. Huge variances exist in the quality and quantity of computer education in our public schools. Some "model" or "magnet" schools have the latest equipment, modern infrastructure and wiring, excellent teacher training, and the beginnings of an integrated curriculum. But this is not the norm. Many schools are counted as being on-line when one computer in the teacher's lounge has a modem.

Schools across the country are trying to step up to the technological revolution, but the results have been uneven and, in many cases, inadequate. Technology education is a complex challenge facing school districts that are already strapped for resources. Yet incorporating technology into the classroom is imperative to prepare students for their lives in the twenty-first century.

Each of the episodes in the "Digital Divide" television series, and each of the chapters in this book, look at a different facet of technology's impact on young people in America and as such this series should be available for educators, activists, and parents nationwide. Everyone connected with the series and the book believes strongly in the power of digital technology to improve the world we live in. However, the problems created by digital technology have been ignored for too long. We hope that we have contributed to this crucial discussion in an important and thoughtful manner.

Experts Interviewed for Digital Divide

ERNEST ADAMS has developed interactive entertainment for ten years. He is currently an audio/video producer for Electronic Arts. Among his credits are "Rabbit Jack's Casino," an early on-line game for AOL; "Third Degree," a multiplayer party game; and the highly successful "Madden NFL Football" simulation. Mr. Adams was also a founder of the Computer Game Developers' Association and is a regular speaker at the annual Game Developers' Conference. He writes a monthly column on game design for the industry webzine *Gamasutra* (www.gamasutra.com). Throughout his career, Mr. Adams has encouraged the game industry to take girls and women seriously as customers; to better the working conditions of women in the industry; and to improve the way that women are portrayed in computer games.

ANDREW BLAU is program director for the Markle Foundation in New York City. He is the former director of communications policy for The Benton Foundation (authors of *The Learning Connection—Schools in the Information Age*), where he was a research and policy expert on educational technology. He was the principal organizer of the Public Interest Summit, the first national meeting that brought together leaders from non-profits, foundations, and the Clinton Administration to discuss public interest policies in communications.

Before joining Benton, Mr. Blau worked with such public interest groups as the Electronic Frontier Foundation, the Alliance for Community Media, and the United Church of Christ on a range of issues including internet policy, the break up of the Bell system, public television, broadcast licensing, and cable regulation. He has testified before Congress about the role of non-profits in the information age, serves on the Executive Committee of the Urban Libraries Council, and is an advisor to Microsoft's "Libraries Online!" initiative to bring networked computers to public libraries.

A native of Belgium, **BART DECREM** graduated from Stanford Law School in 1992. He then received an Echoing Green fellowship to start Plugged In. As executive director of Plugged In, he assumed overall management for the organization until February 1998, when he started focusing more on long-term strategic efforts for the organization. Mr. Decrem is also the chair of the steering committee for the Community Technology Centers Network.

TRISH MILLINES DZIKO spent the first twenty-three years of her life in New Jersey, where she was raised by a single mother who died when Trish was seventeen. She received a computer science degree from Monmouth University in 1979. Her journey to find the right niche in an ever-changing field has taken Ms. Millines Dziko to Philadelphia, Tucson, San Francisco, and

Seattle. For fifteen years, she has been a software tester, a software developer, a manager, a consultant, and a database designer in such industries as military weapons, business systems, communications, and medical equipment. In August of 1996, Ms. Millines Dziko left corporate America and, with the help and support of family, friends, and professional peers, the Technology Access Foundation (TAF) was born. TAF has a mission of bringing technology to communities of color, focusing on students aged eighteen and under.

B. KEITH FULTON is the director of technology programs and policy for the National Urban League. He is the senior advisor for the programs and technology policy direction of both the National Urban League and its 115 local affiliates. In this post, he develops corporate internet strategy, manages NUL publishing to the World Wide Web and other electronic forums, and manages the development and national proliferation of state-of-the-art Technology Education and Access Centers. The mission of Mr. Fulton's work is to bring the benefits of information and communications technologies to underserved communities by integrating emerging technologies into the business of the Urban League affiliates and similarly situated community-based organizations (CBOs), as well as through support for policymakers and practitioners in the technology field. Mr. Fulton is also the founder and chairman of Techni-Coach, a commercial technology integration firm. In January of 1998, Mr. Fulton accepted a role as the sole technology columnist for *The Black World Today*, an African-American news and information source at www.tbwt.com.

JANE M. HEALY, Ph.D, is the author of *Failure to Connect—How Computers Affect Our Children's Minds—for Better and Worse* (1998, Simon and Schuster), and has been an educational psychologist and professional educator for more than thirty-five years, with experience as a classroom teacher, college professor, reading and learning specialist, and elementary school administrator. The author of three previous books, including *Endangered Minds: Why Children Don't Think and What We Can Do about It,* she is a frequent guest on National Public Radio's "Parents' Journal" and a lecturer and consultant to public and private schools and parent groups.

DONNA L. HOFFMAN is an associate professor of marketing and electronic commerce at Vanderbilt University and the co-director of Project 2000, a corporate-sponsored research center devoted to the study of commercializing emerging media like the World Wide Web. Ms. Hoffman's research focuses on internet marketing and electronic commerce, and she works closely with a wide variety of businesses on these issues. She has been a visiting scholar at Interval Research Corporation in Palo Alto every summer since 1995. Ms. Hoffman founded Owen's pioneering MBA program in electronic commerce. She has published widely in marketing and electronic commerce journals and serves on the editorial boards of many major marketing journals. In addition, she was the editor of a special issue of *Marketing Science* on "Marketing and the Internet." In October 1998, Ms. Hoffman was appointed to the Socio-economic and Workforce Panel of President Clinton's Information Technology Advisory Committee.

LARRY IRVING was most recently the assistant secretary of commerce for communications and information and administrator of the National Telecommunications and Information Administration (NTIA). Under Mr. Irving's leadership, NTIA has led or participated in trade missions and conferences in all corners of the world to promote principles of competition, liberalization, and privatization of telecommunications and information sectors. The NTIA in particular has focused on ensuring more equitable access to telecommunications and information technologies for developing and lesser-developed countries. Mr. Irving was named one of the fifty most influential persons in the "Year of the Internet" by *Newsweek* magazine. From March 1987 to March 1993, Mr. Irving was the senior counsel to the U.S. House of Representatives Subcommittee on Telecommunications and Finance, where he helped enact the Cable Television Consumer Protection Act of 1992, the Children's Television Act of 1990, and the Television Decoder Circuitry Act of 1990. Mr. Irving holds a J.D. degree from Stanford.

PEGGY ORENSTEIN is the author of *SchoolGirls: Young Women, Self-Esteem and the Confidence Gap*, an account of the external and internal hurdles facing teenage girls in two disparate communities. Her book was named a 1994 notable book of the year by *The New York Times*. An award-winning writer and speaker, her articles on such topics as women in science, gender bias in the media, reproductive rights, and breast cancer have appeared in numerous national magazines and newspapers including *The New York Times, Los Angeles Times, Mother Jones,* and the *New Yorker.* She is currently at work on a book for Random House on life choices among women between the ages of twenty-five and forty-five.

HILARY PENNINGTON is the president of Jobs for the Future. A nationally recognized expert on education and training issues, she has worked with federal and state governments to develop public policies that integrate economic and human resource development. One of the chief architects of the American School-to-Work movement, Ms. Pennington served on the presidential transition team of the U.S. Departments of Labor and Education in 1992, advised federal policymakers on the development of the School to Work Opportunities Act of 1994, and now serves as a member of the National Advisory Council on School-to-Work Opportunities. In addition to her work with U.S. states and localities, Ms. Pennington has conducted comparative studies of workforce development systems in Europe and South Africa. She is sought internationally as a speaker and advisor on issues of economic security, education reform, workforce development, and corporate responsibility, and has assisted non-profit organizations and corporate foundations with strategic planning and evaluation on these issues. She serves on a number of commissions and task forces, including the Committee for Economic Development.

ROBERT B. REICH is currently the Distinguished University Professor of Social and Economic Policy at Brandeis University. As the nation's twenty-second secretary of labor between 1993 and 1997, he championed many initiatives to better the job prospects for American workers, including advocating appropriate leave for family and medical circumstances, continuing education, and on-the-job training to upgrade the skill set of and improve conditions for all American workers. Previous to this, he served in the Carter and Ford administrations. Mr. Reich is the author of several best-selling books, among them *The Work of Nations: Preparing Ourselves for 21st-Century Capitalism*; *The Next American Frontier*; and *Locked in the Cabinet.*

KRISTI RENNEBOHM-FRANZ has been teaching at Sunnyside Elementary School in Pullman, Washington, since 1990. Prior to that, she taught at the International School in Nairobi, Kenya, and for many years was a cello teacher and speech therapist. While at Sunnyside, Ms. Rennebohm-Franz has also been the school's technology coordinator, and in 1997 was a visiting scholar at the Harvard University Graduate School of Education.

Since 1994 she has been a lead teacher on the International Educational and Resource Network (I*EARN), through which she coordinated the Global Art and Water Habitats Projects. Ms. Rennebohm-Franz's classroom research focuses on literacy and telecommunications, and she is involved in leadership collaborations for educational technology regionally, nationally, and internationally.

WILLIAM L. RUKEYSER's career in news and public information spans more than twenty-five years and includes broadcast, photographic, and print media. He has worked in the United States and overseas. In the last dozen years his concentration has been on political and governmental communications in California. He has been involved in governmental/political communications since 1983. For the last decade, Mr. Rukeyser has worked in Sacramento in a variety of communications capacities for the state department of education, the California Governor's Office of Emergency Services, the Federal Emergency Management Agency, and the gubernatorial campaign of Kathleen Brown. His expertise has been used in designing communications campaigns, informing reporters and editorial boards, and mobilizing public opinion.

Currently, Mr. Rukeyser is coordinator of Learning in the Real World, a non-profit information clearinghouse with a focus on education technology in elementary and secondary schools and the effects of computer use in child cognitive development from birth through age eleven.

JO SANDERS is currently the director of the Center for Gender Equity at Washington Research Institute, which focuses on gender equity training for high-school computer teachers. She has written nine books and dozens of book chapters and articles dealing with gender equity in technology, science, and mathematics, including: *Gender Equity Right from the Start* (1997) and *Lifting the Barriers: 600 Strategies That Really Work to Increase Girls' Participation in Science, Mathematics and Computers* (1994). Through a series of national training programs, Ms. Sanders has taught gender equity skills to thousands of teachers and teacher educators around the world since 1983.

JANESE SWANSON holds several degrees in education, including a doctorate in organization and leadership. Ms. Swanson has co-produced several award-winning titles for Broderbund Software, including "Where in the World is Carmen Sandiego?" and the Playroom/Treehouse series. In addition to these content-rich children's products, Ms. Swanson created several electronic toys through the first company she founded, Kid One For Fun. These include the hit products "TalkBoy FX" from Tiger Electronics, and Yes! Entertainment's Yak Bak series, which has accrued $50 million in retail sales since their introduction in 1994.

OMAR WASOW is the pioneering founder of New York Online, an on-line community begun in 1993 as a more diverse and thoughtful alternative to the commercial services such as AOL. He is also a leading commentator on the challenges and opportunities of new media and the new economy. Tagged by *Newsweek* magazine as one of the fifty most influential people to watch in cyberspace, Mr. Wasow has helped corporate clients like *Consumer Reports*, the *New Yorker*, and Samsung launch successful internet ventures of their own. In addition to running a company full time, Mr. Wasow appears on-air every weekend as the internet analyst for cable channel MSNBC, and every Thursday morning for NBC's flagship TV station in New York, WNBC. Mr. Wasow is on the Board of Contributors for *U.S.A Today*, writes a monthly column for FeedMag.com, and is a Rockefeller Foundation fellow in the Next Generation Leadership program.

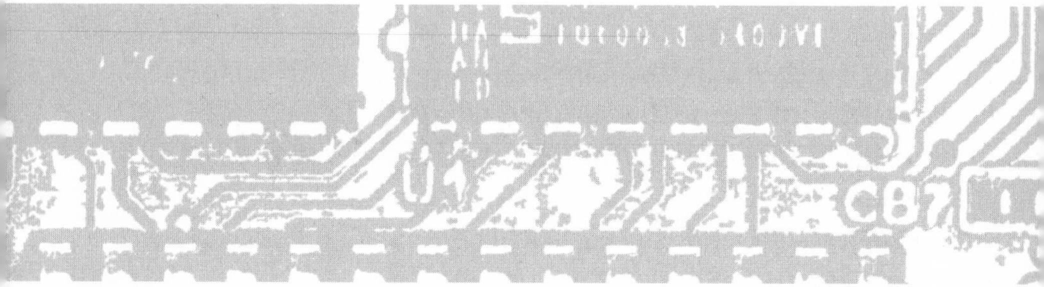

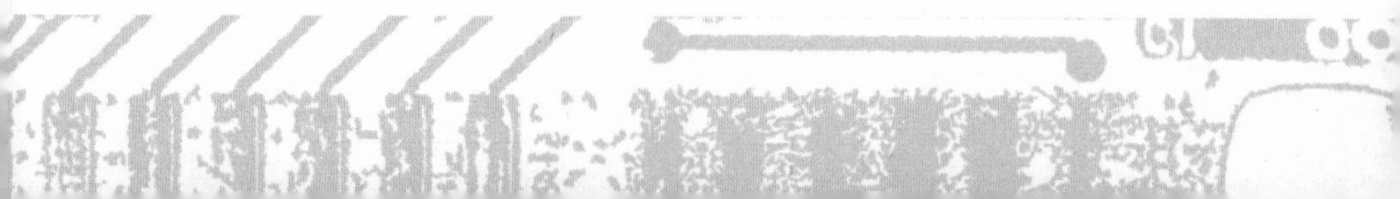

Internet
Resources
for
Digital Divide

The following resources are provided as examples of available materials with an on-line presence. These examples are not meant to be exhaustive, as new materials appear on the internet on a daily basis. As some readers may know, the internet is a far more ephemeral medium than many others. It is therefore likely—to the point of certainty—that more than one of the resources listed here will have moved to a new location, now appear under a different name, or have disappeared altogether between the time this book was written and the time that you read it. While every effort has been made to determine the accessibility of the websites mentioned here at the time of writing, the authors are unable to control or guarantee whether any individual website will be extant at the time of reading. The information provided with each listing should, however, be of great help to the reader in using one or more of the many search engines available on the internet to pursue further research on the associated topics.

Education and Employment

- The Global Art Project (pg. 45) is part of a growing educational trend toward "electronic field trips": students either participate in interactive studies with students from around the world or vicariously accompany travelers on their expeditions. Some sites springing up to support these educational ventures include:

  The Odyssey: World Trek for Service and Education
  (http://www.worldtrek.org/odyssey/index.html)

  GlobaLearn (http://www.globalearn.com)

  The Jason Project (http://www.jasonproject.org)

  Classroom Connect (http://www.classroom.com)

- As the first studies on the effect that all of this technology is actually having on student performance are published, some interesting and perhaps surprising results are surfacing. An on-line newsletter of the National Education Goals Panel cited a study done by the Educational Testing Service last year, noting that those fourth and eighth grade students who spent more time on computers actually did worse on math tests than those who had less time on the computer. The study professed to offer "the first solid evidence of what works and what doesn't when computers are used in the nation's classrooms." The study also indicated that computer technology is most useful when the educators are well-trained on the integration of the technology into an educational plan.

  (http://www.negp.gov/issues/issu/weekly/sep30-98.htm)

- Some progress is being made in examining the state's role in the use of educational technology and what assistance the state can provide. An example of a website examining these issues is the Texas Center for Educational Technology, run through North Texas University, which lists a number of initiatives and projects being operated under its auspices or in conjunction with it, as well as a lengthy list of links to additional resources. It is located at:
  www.tect.unt.edu

- National organizations which support educational professionals are just beginning to address how to use this equipment in the classroom and what training may be necessary for teachers in order to fully utilize this technology. The set of Regional Educational Laboratories, which can be accessed at www.relnetwork.org, contains much information on integrating educational technology into the classroom. One of them, the North Central Regional Laboratory, contains a set of useful materials for educators under the heading of Learning Through Technology at:
  www.ncrel.org/tandl/homepg.htm

- On more local levels, information, expertise, and innovation appear to be driven haphazardly, rather than by an overarching design. This would appear to indicate that decision makers at this level are still learning how to integrate computer and communications technology into the curriculum. Examples of some resources at this level would include The Institute for Learning Technology at Columbia University (www.ilt.Columbia.edu), a cooperative of schools coordinated by a non-profit organization (www.starschools.org), and the journal *From Now On: The Educational Technology Journal*, whose Summer 1999 issue at www.fno.org deals with the question of reluctant or late adopters of this technology.

• Children with special needs also seem to end up on the wrong side of the digital divide. Though mandates to provide physical access to spaces and services have existed for some time now, it is only recently that the on-line needs of individuals with special requirements are even being discussed, let alone dealt with. Recently, the World Wide Web Consortium (W3C), an international internet standards group, announced guidelines on the design and development of websites that embrace access for the physically disabled.
(http://www.w3.org/TR/1999/WAI-WEBCONTENT-19990505/)

Education Statistics and Information

EDUCATIONAL TESTING SERVICE (ETS)
www.ets.org/
The primary source of all standardized educational tests in U.S. public schools (SAT, AP, GRE, etc.). ETS also conducts research regarding trends in education and educational technology.

NATIONAL CENTER FOR EDUCATION STATISTICS
www.nces.ed.gov/

NCES is the arm of the U.S. Department of Education that collects data and publishes reports about the state of U.S. education. Their website is an excellent resource for current statistics on technology in schools and related demographics.

Community Training

ALLIANCE FOR COMMUNITY MEDIA
www.alliancecm.org/

666 11th Street, NW, Suite 806
Washington, DC 20001-4542
phone: 202-393-2650

The Alliance for Community Media is a national organization focusing on equal access to electronic media. It provides technical assistance, promotes successful applications of technology, and serves as an advocate for support to its members, which include 950 public, educational, and government access centers.

BREAK AWAY TECHNOLOGIES
www.breakaway.org/

3417 W. Jefferson Boulevard
Los Angeles, CA 90018
phone: 213-737-7677
fax: 213-299-8226

Break Away Technologies is a fifteen thousand square-foot access center in South Central Los Angeles that uses donated computers to provide technology classes for neighborhood residents and area schools. Break Away also teaches leadership and responsibility in efforts to facilitate students entering the increasingly technological, team-based workplace.

COMMUNITY TECHNOLOGY CENTERS NETWORK (CTCNET)
www.ctcnet.org/
>   55 Chapel Street
>   Newton, MA 02158
>   phone: 617-969-7100
>   fax: 617-332-4318
>   e-mail: ctcnet@edc.org

CTCNet is a clearinghouse organization for the more than 250 computer access centers in the United States. The centers partner with schools, museums, community centers, and churches to promote equitable access to technology.

COMPUTERS IN OUR FUTURE
www.igc.org/compfuture/
>   3580 Wilshire Boulevard, Suite 1660
>   Los Angeles, CA 90010
>   phone: 213-368-2373
>   fax:213-368-2371
>   e-mail: ciof@aol.com

Computers in Our Future is a five-year initiative charged with developing eleven community computer training centers in low-income neighborhoods across California.

WOMEN'S ECONOMIC AGENDA PROJECT (WEAP)
www.weap.org/
> 449 Fifteenth Street, 2nd floor
> Oakland, CA 94612
> phone: 510-451-7379
> fax: 510-968-8628
> e-mail: weap@sirius.com

WEAP provides access to high-tech equipment and applications for women and minority-owned businesses. A computer training program offers basic, intermediate, and advanced computer training to prepare low-income women and minorities for well-paying jobs and better careers.

Jobs and Income

EMPLOYMENT PROJECTIONS
stats.bls.gov/empbib01.htm
> Bureau of Labor Statistics
> Division of Information Services
> 2 Massachusetts Ave. NE, Rm. 2860
> Washington, DC 20212
> phone: 202-606-5886
> fax: 202-606-7890
> e-mail: blsdata_staff@bls.gov
> or various others available through the
> website at: stats.bls.gov/hlpcont.htm

This is the Bureau of Labor Statistics website, forecasting the employment outlook through 2006, including the Monthly

Labor Review. Includes listings of hot and not-so-hot jobs, their earning potential, and other demographics.

JOBS FOR THE FUTURE
www.jff.org/
> 88 Broad St., 8th Fl.
> Boston, MA 02110
> phone: 617-728-4446
> fax: 617-728-4857
> e-mail: info@jff.org

The goal of Jobs for the Future is to devise and disseminate strategies that engage young people and adults in their learning and equip them to shape their futures through community-based programs geared at getting young adults into the workforce with all the necessary technological tools.

THE STATE OF WORKING AMERICA 1996-97 BY LAWRENCE MISHEL, JARED BERNSTEIN, AND JOHN SCHMITT, ECONOMIC POLICY INSTITUTE
epinet.org
> 1660 L St. NW, Suite 1200
> Washington, DC 20036
> phone: 202-775-8810
> fax: 202-775-0819
> e-mail: publications@epinet.org

A site containing a detailed report on wages and how they correlate to education levels, for review or purchase.

Research

BENTON FOUNDATION
www.benton.org/
1634 Eye Street, NW
Washington, DC 20006
phone: 202-638-5770
e-mail: cpp@benton.org

The Benton Foundation is an organization for research, policy analysis, and print, video, and on-line publishing, as well as an outreach organization to non-profits and foundations. It has updates on communications policy and events, a forum for discussion, and working papers, not to mention links to hundreds of on-line communications and public interest resources. The Benton Foundation also has a weekly list service called "Up for Grabs," which may be subscribed to at the e-mail address: UPFORGRABS-L@CDINET.COM. This mailing list delivers e-mail updates on all Benton activities and issues.

BUREAU OF LABOR STATISTICS NEWS RELEASES
stats.bls.gov/newsrels.htm
Bureau of Labor Statistics
Division of Information Services
2 Massachusetts Ave. NE, Rm. 2860
Washington, DC 20212
phone: 202-606-5886
fax: 202-606-7890
e-mail: blsdata_staff@bls.gov or various
others available through the website at:
stats.bls.gov/hlpcont.htm

This government website provides access to various research and statistical information on earnings and jobs. These releases are regularly updated.

EDUCATIONAL DEVELOPMENT CENTER (EDC)/CENTER FOR CHILDREN AND TECHNOLOGY (CCT)
www.edc.org/
> 96 Morton Street
> New York, NY 10014
> phone: 212-807-4200
> fax: 212-633-8804

The center conducts research on how different societal groups perceive technology. One of EDC's projects, Access by Design, develops approaches for increasing access to under-represented groups.

HIGH TECHNOLOGY AND LOW-INCOME COMMUNITIES: PROSPECTS FOR THE POSITIVE USE OF ADVANCED INFORMATION TECHNOLOGY BY DONALD A. SCHON, BISH SANYAL, AND WILLIAM J. MITCHELL, MIT UNIVERSITY PRESS
mitpress.mit.edu/book-home.tcl?isbn=026269199X
> The MIT Press
> Five Cambridge Center
> Cambridge, MA 02142
> phone: 617-253-5646
> fax: 617-258-6779
> e-mail: books@mit.edu

This book is a collection of papers that takes a practical yet critical look at the potential impacts of technology on cities,

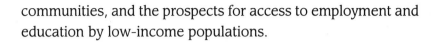

communities, and the prospects for access to employment and education by low-income populations.

NIELSEN MEDIA RESEARCH
www.nielsenmedia.com/
299 Park Ave.
New York, NY 10171
phone: 212-708-7500
fax: 212-708-7795
e-mail: Through the website

This is a research website with loads of demographics on technology users, incomes, trends, etc.

Expert Contacts

BART DECREM may be contacted through:
Plugged In
1923 University Avenue
East Palo Alto, CA 94303
phone: 650-322-1134 Ext. 21
e-mail: bartd@pluggedin.org
website: http://www.pluggedin.org

LARRY IRVING may be contacted through:
Irving Information Group
1225 Eye St. NW
Suite 350
Washington, DC 20005

HILARY PENNINGTON may be contacted through:
> Jobs for the Future
> 88 Broad Street
> Boston, MA 02110
> phone: 617-728-4446
> e-mail: hpenning@jff.org
> website: http://www.jff.org

ROBERT B. REICH may be contacted through:
> Brandeis University
> Heller School, P.O. Box 9110
> Waltham, MA 02254-9110
> phone: 781-736-3850
> fax: 781-736-3482
> e-mail: Reich@brandeis.edu
> website: http://www.brandeis.edu

Gender

CHICKCLICK
> **www.chickclick.com/**

A network of "independent, girl-powered websites. . . . Girl sites that don't fake it." Their site links have included: RiotGrrl; GrrlGamer; Fresh and Tasty Women's Snowboarding; Swanky; Go, Girl!; and many others.

FEMINA
> **www.femina.com/**

This website contains a great directory of women's resources on the web, compiled by internet marketing consultant Aliza Sherman, creator of the Cybergrrl site.

GIRLS INCORPORATED
www.girlsinc.org

A national youth organization dedicated to helping every girl become strong, smart, and bold, Girls Inc. has been providing vital educational programs to millions of girls in the United States for more than fifty years. Current programs with Girls Inc. are aimed at helping girls confront subtle societal stereotypes about their value and potential and at preparing them to lead successful, independent lives.

GIRL POWER INFO AND RESOURCES
www.girlpower.com/info.htm

Contains a listing of resources and addresses for a variety of topics that may be of interest to girls; no links.

GIRL TECH
www.girltech.com

Girl Tech is an award-wining website with over four hundred pages of fun educational content. Featuring games, an advice column, a weekly diary, women role models, science projects, inventions, sports, and a boys' area designed to encourage communication and understanding between girls and boys.

PLANET GIRL BY GIRL GAMES INC.
www.planetgirl.com/

An entertainment company designing and developing innovative products, including interactive CD-ROMs, on-line environments, research and development, broadcasts, and toys for girls eight to eighteen years old.

PURPLE MOON
web.purple-moon.com/

A safe, highly interactive, and entertaining place for girls to have their very own "Friendship Adventures" on-line. Characters such as Rockett take girls on scavenger hunts, let them write stories and vote on new ideas, and teach girls how to create their own web pages.

SMARTGRRLS
www.smartgrrls.org/

Founded in 1997 by Rachel Muir with little more than five hundred dollars and a credit line, SmartGrrls has now become one of the definitive sites for girls on the web, devoted to giving hands-on instruction and providing role models in math, science, and engineering. Terry Hiner is now associated with SmartGrrls as its Program Director.

SUPERKIDS EDUCATIONAL SOFTWARE REVIEW
www.superkids.com/aweb/pages/features/girls

Contains several articles on girls and technology, as well as reviews of over thirty software products for girls.

WEBGRRLS
www.webgrrls.com/

An international networking group of women involved in

projects dealing with the internet, CD-ROMs, and other electronic media. It provides a forum for women in, or interested in, new media and technology, with emphases on networking, exchanging job and business leads, forming strategic alliances, teaching and mentoring, internships, and learning the skills needed to succeed in an increasingly technical workplace and world.

WOMEN'S WIRE
www.womenswire.com

An on-line magazine concentrating on issues important to women. Their website includes daily news stories about women, profiles of prominent women, and a list of women-focused web resources dealing with careers, health, and personal issues.

Technology and Gender Equity

AMERICAN ASSOCIATION OF UNIVERSITY WOMEN
www.aauw.org/

This organization is devoted to promoting equity and education for all women and girls. Several landmark studies on how young girls are subtly steered away from academic success, including success in math and science, have been published under its auspices. Their website gives summaries of the studies and information on how to order copies by mail or phone. Their recent study on gender gaps is very thorough.

Carnegie Mellon Gender Equity & C++ Training
www.cs.cmu.edu/6apt/

A website devoted to instructing teachers on how to use and teach the C++ language, which will be introduced in the 1999 Computer Science Advanced Placement exam in all high schools. The site also discusses how to establish and maintain gender equity in the classroom and computer lab in order to attract and retain female students in computing courses.

Committee on the Status of Women in Computer Science and Engineering, from the Computing Research Association (CRA-W)
www.cra.org/Activities/craw/

Funded by the National Science Foundation and other sources, this organization is dedicated to increasing the number of women involved in CSE, seeks to increase the degree of success they experience in these fields, and provides a forum for addressing problems that women experience in these fields. In addition to involvement with other professional organizations at conferences, CRA-W sponsors mentoring workshops at various computer science conferences, the "Expanding the Pipeline" columns in *Computing Research News*, the Systers-Academia electronic network, the development and maintenance of a database of Ph.D. women in CSE, and the Distributed Mentoring project. The current co-chairs of the committee are Jan Cuny (cuny@cs.uoregon.edu), University of Oregon, and Leah Jamieson (lhj@ecn.purdue.edu), Purdue University.

INSTITUTE FOR WOMEN AND TECHNOLOGY
www.iwt.org

An organization creating opportunities for women to discuss and to participate fully in the creation of new technologies.

WOMEN'S ECONOMIC AGENDA PROJECT (WEAP)
www.weap.org/

    449 Fifteenth Street, 2nd floor

    Oakland, CA 94612

    phone: 510-451-7379

    fax: 510-968-8628

    e-mail: weap@sirius.com

Women in the Computer Industry

INTERNATIONAL NETWORK OF WOMEN IN TECHNOLOGY (WITI)
www.witi.com/index-c.shtml

This association of women working in high-tech fields has a website that includes membership information, the electronic text of the federal Glass Ceiling Report on women and minorities in corporate management, and a list of other on-line resources for women in the technology field.

SYSTERS
www-anw.cs.umass.edu/~amy/systers.html

Systers-students is a mailing list open to all female graduate and undergraduate students studying computer science and related areas.

Expert Contacts

ERNEST ADAMS may be contacted through:
    Electronic Arts
    e-mail: eadams@ea.com
    website: http://www.ea.com

PEGGY ORENSTEIN may be contacted:
    c/o Sandra Dijkstra Literary Agency
    1155 Camino Del Mar, 515#
    Del Mar, CA 92014
    e-mail: pjorenstein@mindspring.com

JO SANDERS may be contacted through:
    Center for Gender Equity
    Washington Research Institute
    150 Nickerson Street, Suite 305
    Seattle, WA 98109
    phone: 206-285-9317
    fax: 206-285-1523
    e-mail: jsanders@wri-edu.org
    website: http://www.wri-edu.org/equity

JANESE SWANSON may be contacted through:
    Girl Tech

1537 Fourth Street, Suite 189
San Rafael, CA 94901
phone: 415-256-1510
fax: 415-256-1515
e-mail: grltek@aol.com
website: http://www.girltech.com

Race

COMMUNITY TECHNOLOGY CENTERS NETWORK (CTCNET)
www.ctcnet.org/
55 Chapel Street
Newton, MA 02158
phone: 617-969-7100
fax: 617-332-4318
e-mail: ctcnet@edc.org

EAST HARLEM TUTORIAL PROGRAM (EHTP)
www.east-harlem.com/ehtp.htm

This organization supports students in all forms of learning programs, technical and otherwise, as they reach, strive, struggle, and ultimately succeed. EHTP believes that support depends on developing the capacities of every member of the EHTP extended family: the students, their parents, and the EHTP guardians, volunteers, staff, trustees, and donors.

LATINOLINK

www.latinolink.com

A weekly magazine with news, columns, and other items of interest to Latinos in the U.S.

NATIONAL URBAN LEAGUE

www.nul.org/

The United States' premier social and civil rights organization, it has championed technology-based initiatives in low-income communities since 1968 and promotes advocacy and program services for the social and educational development of youth, economic independence, and racial equality. The Urban League has 115 affiliates in 34 states.

ORACLE'S PROMISE

www.oracle.com/promise/livehtml/index.html

A philanthropic initiative of Oracle Corporation, chartered to provide network computers to economically challenged, disenfranchised public schools. The initiative was unveiled in 1997, when Oracle Corporation announced a $100 million donation to be used for providing network computer access to every schoolchild in America.

PERISCOPIO

www.periscopio.com

One of the leading Spanish-language websites providing news and communication resources to the Latino community.

PICOSITO

www.picosito.com

The leading internet community for U.S. Hispanics/Latinos, providing high quality branded channels of information, communication resources, and shopping services in English and Spanish.

PLUGGED IN, INC.

www.pluggedin.org/

A non-profit company in one of Silicon Valley's poorest communities, Plugged In runs an after-school program for elementary school children and offers classes and work-preparation experience for teenagers in numerous technology areas.

TECHNOLOGY ACCESS FOUNDATION (TAF)

www.techaccess.org/

This is a non-profit agency, whose stated mission is to provide communities of color access to technology. This organization is the brainchild of Microsoft retiree Trish Millines Dziko and former Seattle Mental Health practitioner Jill Hull. TAF was started in October 1996 to educate communities about the role of technology in their present and future.

URBAN TECHNOLOGY CENTER

www.urbantech.org/

A non-profit corporation dedicated to preparing inner-city communities across the country for full participation in the information age by creating a technology and telecommunications infrastructure.

Research, Surveys and Statistics

BRIDGING THE DIGITAL DIVIDE: THE IMPACT OF RACE
    ON COMPUTER ACCESS AND INTERNET USE, BY
    THOMAS P. NOVAK AND DONNA L. HOFFMAN,
    PROJECT 2000, VANDERBILT UNIVERSITY,
    FEBRUARY 2, 1998
    ecommerce.vanderbilt.edu/papers/race/science.html
    A comprehensive report analyzing the demographic pat-
terns of internet access and computer usage from late 1996 to
early 1997. It endeavors to produce a systematic examination
of the differences between African-Americans and European-
Americans in the U.S. with regard to the influence of education
and income on technological access.

BUILDINGS, BOOKS AND BYTES: LIBRARIES AND
    COMMUNITIES IN THE DIGITAL AGE, THE BENTON
    FOUNDATION, NOVEMBER 1996
    www.benton.org/Library/Kellogg/buildings.html
    A report on how libraries can help communities move into
the digital age.

CLOSING THE DIGITAL DIVIDE: ENHANCING HISPANIC
    PARTICIPATION IN THE INFORMATION AGE, BY
    ANTHONY WILHELM, TOMAS RIVERA POLICY
    INSTITUTE, APRIL 1998
    www.trpi.org/publications.html
    This report is a study on computer ownership and use
among Hispanics between 1994 and 1998.

COMPUTER INTELLIGENCE
www.ci.zd.com/

A source of fact-based information on computer and communications industry trends and activities.

COMPUTERS AND CLASSROOMS: THE STATUS OF TECHNOLOGY IN U.S. SCHOOLS, EDUCATIONAL TESTING SERVICE (ETS), 1997
www.ets.org/research/pic/compclass.html

A report providing a snapshot of the use and effectiveness of technology in American schools. You can purchase printed copies of the report for $9.50 or view an electronic copy on the ETS website.

FALLING THROUGH THE NET
www.ntia.doc.gov/ntiahome/fttn99

The annual study conducted by the U.S. Department of Commerce, providing comprehensive data on the level of access by Americans to telephones, computers, and the internet.

NUA SURVEYS
www.nua.ie/surveys/

NUA is a service that gathers internet-related data and demographics from a variety of sources and posts them on their website. It also supports a mailing list with weekly updates of various internet usage information, focusing on the number of people that are on-line.

**"WEB USERS ARE LOOKING MORE LIKE AMERICANS,"
BY DAVID BIRDSELL, DOUGLAS MUZZIO, DAVID
KRANE, AND AMY COTTREAU IN *THE PUBLIC
PERSPECTIVE*, APRIL/MAY 1998**

www.ropercenter.uconn.edu/pubper/pdf/pp93b.pdf

This is a study that found that the population accessing the internet is beginning to reflect the diversity of the general population. The report notes that there are still differences, though, in the areas of education and income: web users are still more likely to be people with college degrees and incomes of at least $50,000, and adults with a high-school education or less account for only 19 percent of web users.

Expert Contacts

TRISH MILLINES DZIKO

Co-founder and Executive Director
Technology Access Foundation
3803 S. Edmunds St., Suite A
Seattle, WA 98118
phone: 206-725-9095
fax: 206-725-9097
e-mail: trishmi@techaccess.org
website: http://www.techaccess.org

B. KEITH FULTON

Director, Technology Programs & Policy
National Urban League
120 Wall Street

New York, NY 10005
phone: 212-558-5394
fax: 212-344-5332
e-mail: bkfulton@nul.org
website: http://www.nul.org

PROFESSOR DONNA L. HOFFMAN

Owen Graduate School of Management
Vanderbilt University.
Nashville, TN 37203
e-mail: donna.hoffman@vanderbilt.edu
website:
http://www2000.ogsm.vanderbilt.edu/

OMAR WASOW

Founder, New York Online
549 Pacific Street
Brooklyn, NY 11217-1902
e-mail: omar@nyo.com
website: http://www.nyo.com

6264 10 P

6 64 10 P

CB7

Appendices

Telephone Access in the U.S.

The graphs in this Appendix indicate where a central part of the digital divide begins, with the nation's telecommunications and information infrastructure. If a household does not have telephone access, it almost certainly does not have internet access. If it does not have internet access, then children in the household are not able to work on internet-based projects at home, widening the gap between them and their connected peers; there is no parent-child interaction to reinforce learning using an internet-connected computer; and students are not able to gain familiarity and facility with the connectivity tools central to commerce in the Information Age.

For all of the following appendices, acknowledgment is made to the U.S. Department of Commerce, National Telecommunications and Information Administration, for the use of these charts and graphs from the 1999 *Falling Through the Net* study. The study, with much more in-depth information, is available at www.ntia.doc.gov/ntiahome/fttn99.

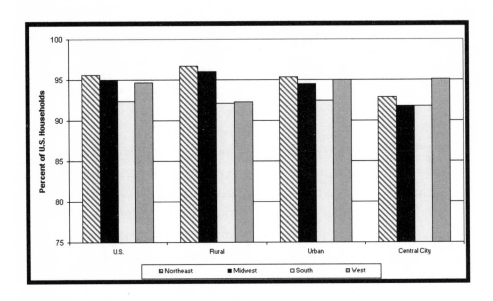

FIGURE 1-1

The percentage of U.S. households that have telephones, broken down by overall U.S. rural, urban, and central (inner) city environments, for different regions of the U.S. for the year 1998. Note that America's inner cities, some of our nation's most impoverished locations, have less home telephones than the most rural areas of the country.

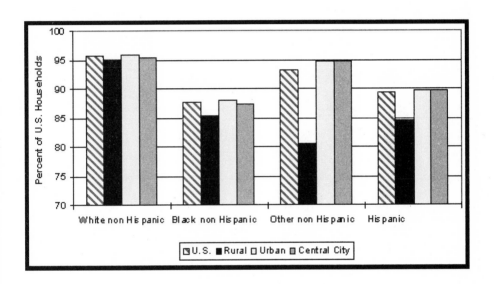

FIGURE 1-2

The percentage of U.S. households that have telephones, broken down by overall U.S., rural, urban, and central (inner) city environments and by race/origin, for the year 1998. One noteworthy point made by this graph is that African-Americans and Hispanic-Americans are at least 5 percentage points below other racial groups in the U.S. for telephone ownership in almost all locations.

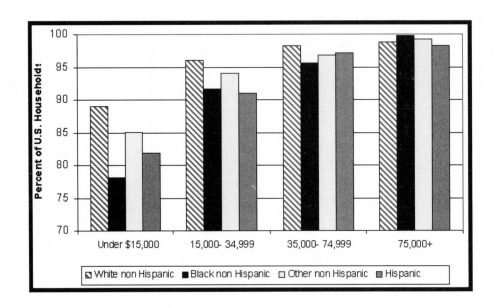

FIGURE 1-3

The percentage of U.S. households that have telephones, broken down by race and income, for the year 1998. As might be expected, the higher the income, the greater the likelihood of having a telephone.

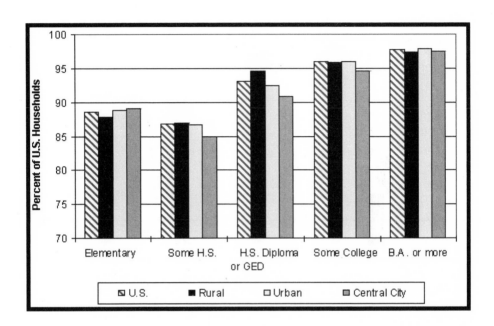

FIGURE 1-4

The percentage of U.S. households that have telephones, broken down by overall U.S., rural, urban, and central (inner) city environments and by educational attainment, for the year 1998. Here, it should be noted that there is a large jump in telephone ownership, even in America's inner cities, with an increase in education. This may, however, be as much a link between ownership and income potential as directly related to education.

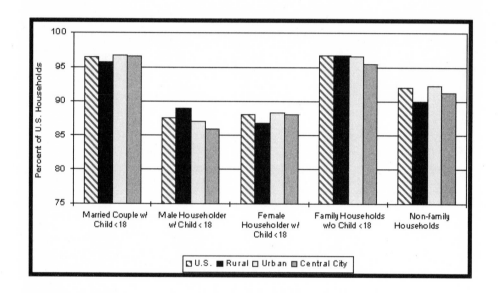

FIGURE 1-5
The percentage of U.S. households that have telephones, broken down by overall U.S., rural, urban, and central (inner) city environments and by household type, for the year 1998. As can be seen by the almost 10 percent gap between them, single-parent households suffer greatly in relation to households with two parents.

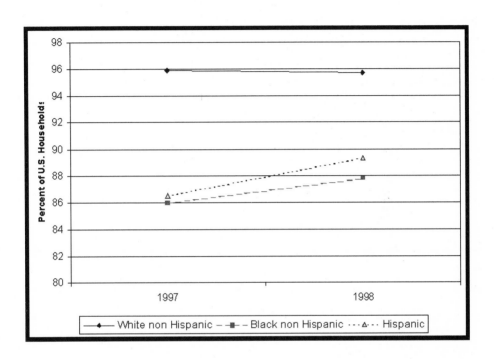

FIGURE 1-6

A comparison by race for telephone ownership between 1997 and 1998. This chart clearly shows the overall gap in home telephone ownership between European-Americans and African- and Hispanic-Americans, as well as indicating that the gap is closing.

Computer Ownership in the U.S.

If a household does not have a computer, it is also unlikely to have internet access. As more schools, homes, and businesses have computers and communications access, we run the risk of assuming that *everyone* has them and further isolating those who do not.

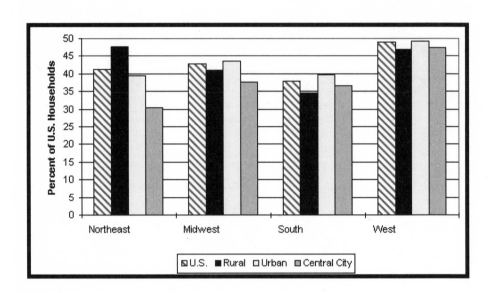

FIGURE 2-1

The percentage of U.S. households that have computers, broken down by overall U.S., rural, urban, and central (inner) city environments, for different regions of the U.S., for the year 1998. This graph indicates a different picture than for telephone ownership, showing that though the country's inner cities still lag nationwide, the West has computers much more evenly distributed and in higher numbers.

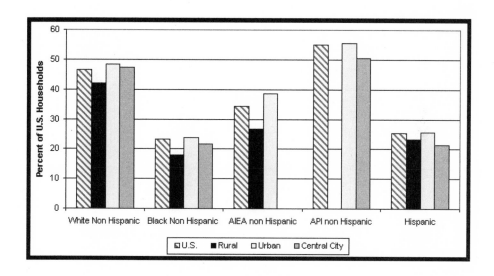

FIGURE 2-2

The percentage of U.S. households that have computers, broken down by overall U.S., rural, urban, and central (inner) city environments and by race/origin, for the year 1998. Again, as with telephone ownership, African- and Hispanic-Americans lag behind other racial groups in the U.S. for computer ownership in almost all locations.

Notes: AIEA stands for American Indian/Eskimo/Aleut, whose bar for
   central city penetration is missing, but is noted on-line as 35.6 percent; API stands for Asian/Pacific Islander, whose bar for rural
   penetration is missing, but is noted on-line as 40.6 percent.

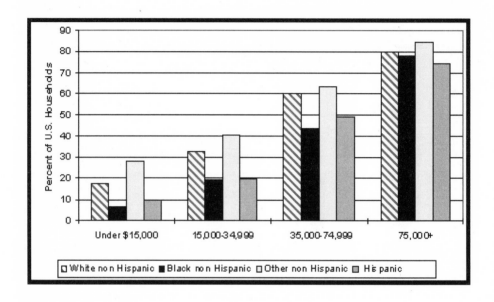

FIGURE 2-3

The percentage of U.S. households that have computers, broken down by race and income, for the year 1998. A clear correlation is shown here between income level and computer ownership, with the gaps closing significantly at the highest income levels.

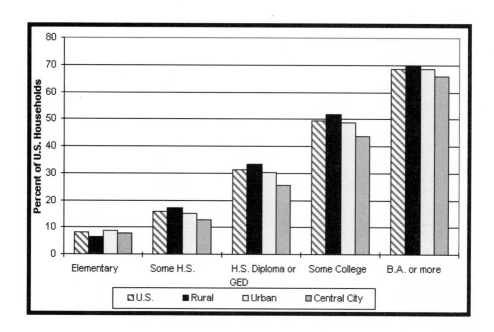

FIGURE 2-4

The percentage of U.S. households that have computers, broken down by overall U.S., rural, urban, and central (inner) city environments and by educational attainment, for the year 1998. Here, it should be noted that there is a huge jump in computer ownership, even in the nation's inner cities, with an increase in education.

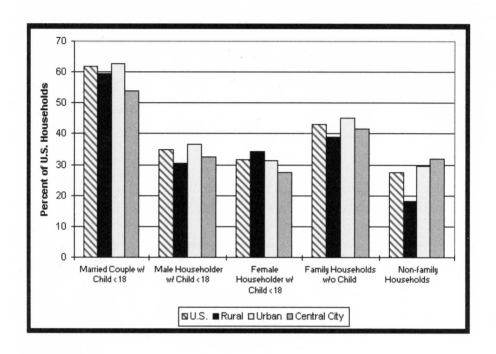

FIGURE 2-5

The percentage of U.S. households that have computers, broken down by overall U.S., rural, urban, and central (inner) city environments and by household type, for the year 1998. The computer-ownership gap between single-parent households and married couples with children is far greater than the telephone-ownership gap, almost 30 percent in one case. The reasons for this bear further scrutiny, and are likely related to resources of all kinds being stretched to the utmost in single-parent homes.

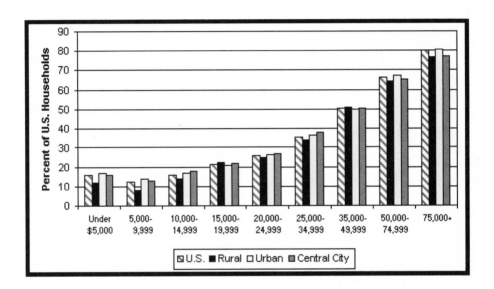

FIGURE 2-6

The percentage of U.S. households that have computers, broken down by overall U.S., rural, urban, and central (inner) city environments and by income, for the year 1998. This graph indicates that computer ownership is much more closely tied to income than to geographic location.

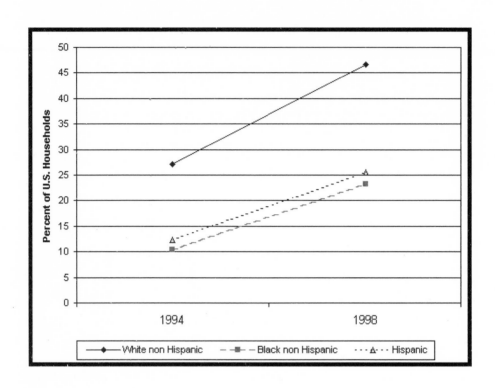

FIGURE 2-7

A comparison by race of home computer ownership between 1994 and 1998. This chart also shows the overall gap, this time in home computer ownership, between European-Americans and African- and Hispanic-Americans, along with the indication that the gap is widening, not closing.

Internet Use in the U.S.

I n this appendix, the graphs show how many people are using the internet, who they are, and where they are located. Just as access to tires and gasoline are necessities for traversing the nation's highways, so too are computer tools and internet access necessities for traveling the nation's Information Superhighway.

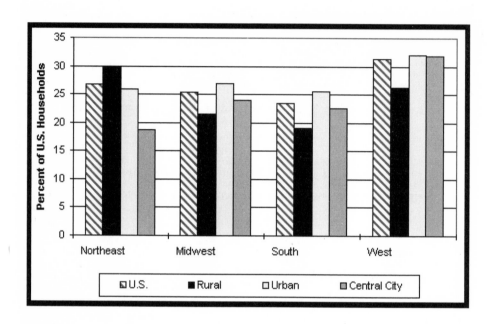

FIGURE 3-1

The percentage of U.S. households that use the internet, broken down by overall U.S., rural, urban, and central (inner) city environments for different U.S. regions, for the year 1998. This graph notes that, as with computer ownership, the West leads the nation. Of interest here is that the nation's inner cities are ahead of the rural areas, everywhere but in the Northeast, where the level of internet use is below that of the rural South.

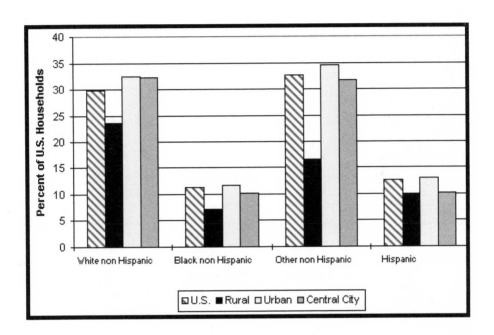

FIGURE 3-2

The percentage of U.S. households that use the internet, broken down by overall U.S., rural, urban, and central (inner) city environments and by race/origin, for the year 1998. It should be noted here that internet use by Hispanic- and African-Americans in *any* environment is below that of rural European-Americans and other racial groups, which would include Native-American on reservations.

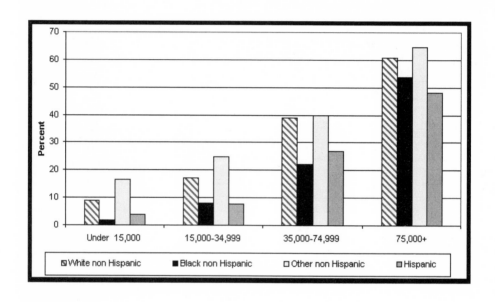

FIGURE 3-3

The percentage of U.S. households that use the internet, broken down by race and income, for the year 1998. Here again, there is a close connection between income level and internet use, as there was for computer ownership, again with the gaps closing at the highest income levels.

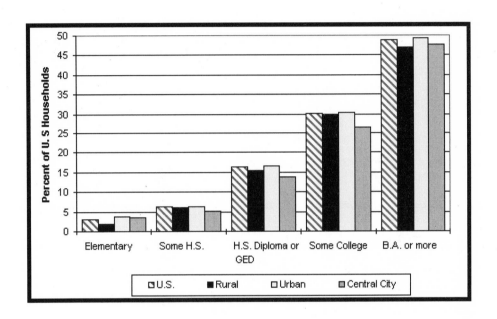

FIGURE 3-4

The percentage of U.S. households that use the internet, broken down by overall U.S., rural, urban, and central (inner) city environments and by educational attainment, for the year 1998. Once again, with an increase in education comes an increase in the use of the tools of the Information Age.

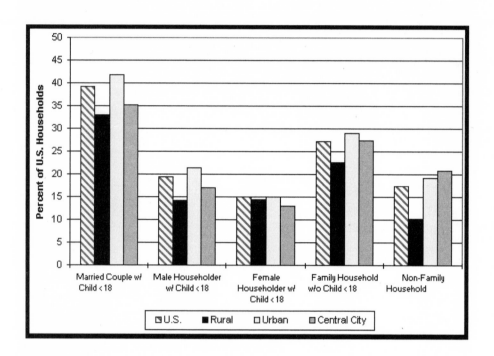

FIGURE 3-5

The percentage of U.S. households that use the internet, broken down by overall U.S., rural, urban, and central (inner) city environments and by household type, for the year 1998. Consistently, we see a gap between single-parent households and those with two parents.

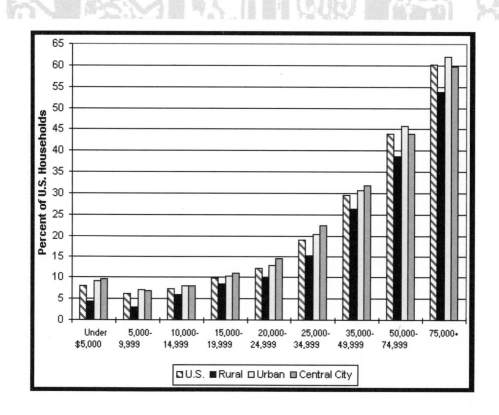

FIGURE 3-6

The percentage of U.S. households that use the internet, broken down by overall U.S., rural, urban, and central (inner) city environments and by income, for the year 1998.

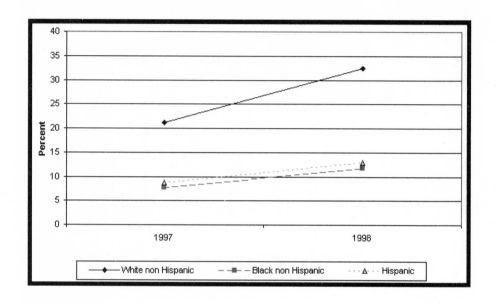

FIGURE 3-7

A chart showing a comparison by race/origin for internet use between 1997 and 1998. This is yet another chart showing not only a racial gap in use, but the fact that this divide is widening.

Internet Use by Location
in the U.S.

It is also important to look at where those people who *are* on the internet are accessing it, and what they are using the internet for. Be aware that the figures in this appendix represent only a small segment of the total population of our nation, as many people have *never* been on-line.

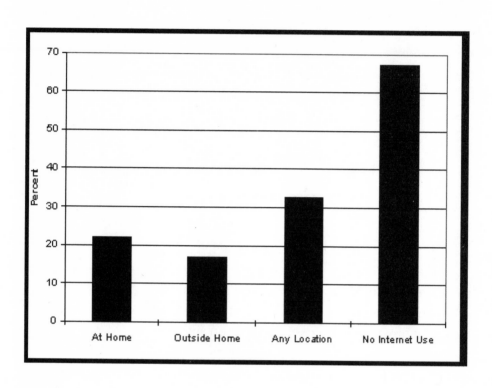

FIGURE 4-1

The percentage of U.S. citizens that use the internet, by use location, for the year 1998. The important point on this graph is the bar on the far right, showing that almost 70 percent of Americans are not on the internet.

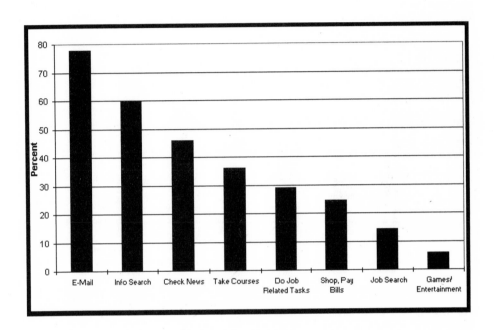

FIGURE 4-2

The percentage of U.S. citizens that use the internet at home, broken down by type of use, for the year 1998. This graph is noteworthy in showing that, at present, commerce and job-searching are far down on the list of functions of the internet at home.

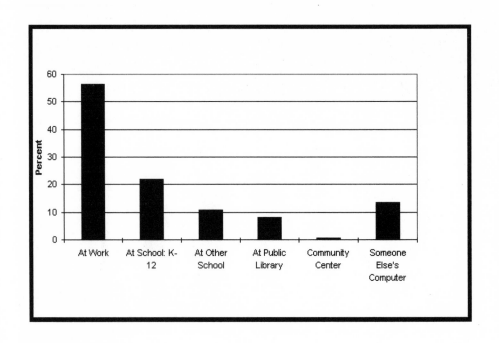

FIGURE 4-3

The percentage of U.S. citizens using the internet outside of the home, broken down by use location, for the year 1998. Interestingly, this graph shows that access at CTCs only represents a tiny fraction of internet access.

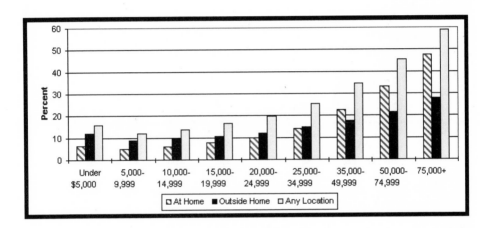

FIGURE 4-4

The percentage of U.S. citizens using the internet, broken down by income and use location, for the year 1998.

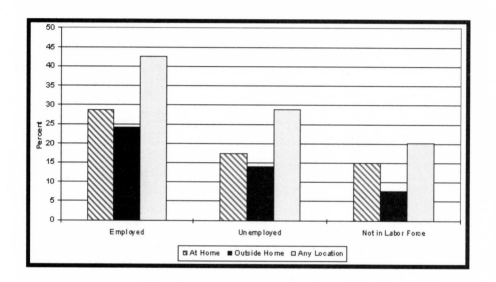

FIGURE 4-5

The percentage of U.S. citizens using the internet, broken down by employment status and use location, for the year 1998. Given that many people indicated internet access at work (Figures 4-3 and 4-6), it is not surprising that the numbers for access among the unemployed drop precipitously.

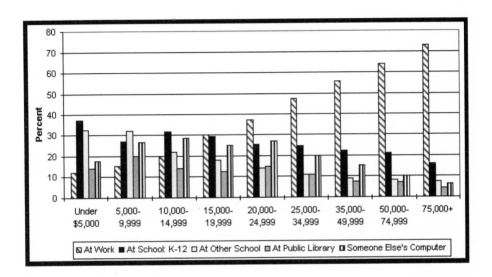

FIGURE 4-6

The percentage of U.S. citizens using the internet outside of the home, broken down by use location and by income, for the year 1998.

Gender Differences in Internet Use in the U.S.

I n this final appendix, we wanted to present a number of graphs denoting gender differences in internet use. This is an area where more study, and more action, is required. It is time to implement greater gender equity in our culture, as noted in this book.

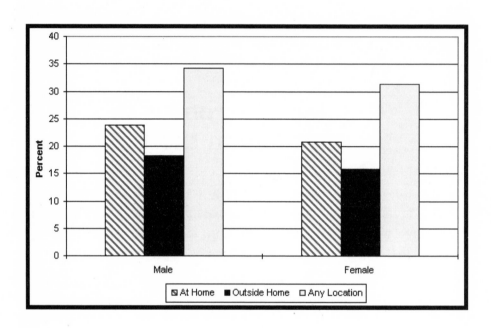

FIGURE 5-1

The percentage of U.S. citizens that use the internet, by gender and use location, for the year 1998. Overall, this graph indicates that women are still less likely than men to be on-line.

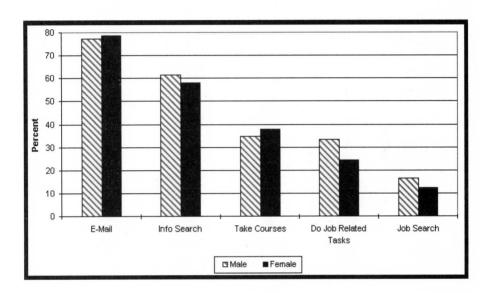

FIGURE 5-2

The percentage of U.S. citizens that use the internet at home, broken down by gender and type of use, for the year 1998. It is noted with some interest that women are more likely to take courses on-line than men are, possibly reflecting an understanding of the disadvantages for them of the classroom gender bias noted in this book.

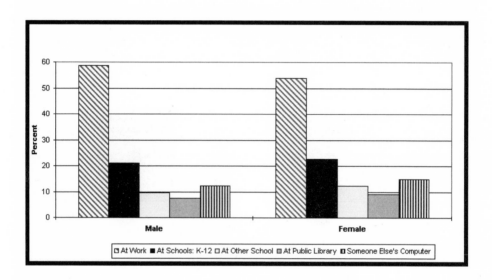

FIGURE 5-3

The percentage of U.S. citizens using the internet outside of the home, broken down by gender and use location, for the year 1998. Interestingly, this graph shows that women are more likely to be on the internet than men at any location other than at work.

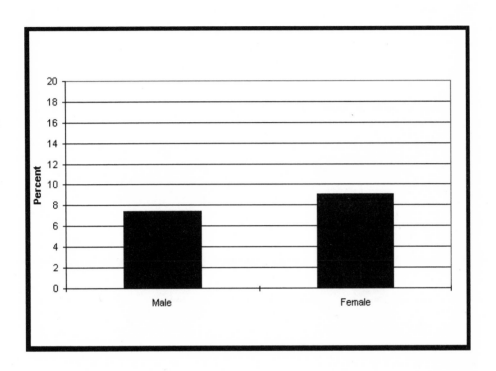

FIGURE 5-4

The percentage of U.S. citizens using the internet, broken down by gender and internet use at libraries, for the year 1998. One reason why more females use library internet resources than males, although the NTIA study does not address this statistical chart directly, is perhaps because they are unable to get sufficient time on-line at schools, in competition with their male peers.

About the
Authors

DAVID **B**OLT is an award-winning documentary film producer with over fifteen years of experience and a special interest in education technology. He has worked on the cutting edge of technology and social issues, including a position directing the technology for the Bay Area Video Coalition, and at George Lucas' Educational Foundation at Skywalker Ranch in Marin County, CA. He is also a founder of the National Coalition of Independent Public Television Producers and a co-founder of Studio Miramar. He lives in San Francisco.

RAY **C**RAWFORD has had a career in technical and educational publishing spanning over twenty years, most recently as a Projects Managing Editor. His interest in history and social issues has led to contributions to both magazines and on-line content. He is a member of several scholarly and literary organizations, including the National Coalition of Independent Scholars. Believing that social activism is everyone's responsibility, Ray has been involved locally as a counseling volunteer and with the local animal shelter. He lives with his partner Karla in San Francisco.